A CENTURY OF WOMEN CARTOONISTS

BY TRINA ROBBINS

Northampton KITCHEN SINK PRESS Massachusetts

Published by Kitchen Sink Press, Inc., 320 Riverside Drive, Northampton MA 01060. Free catalog on request.

Printed in U.S.A.

Library of Congress Cataloging-in-Publication Data
Robbins, Trina.
A Century of Women Cartoonists / by Trina Robbins
p.   cm.
ISBN 0-87816-200-3 (softcover, $16.95)
ISBN 0-87816-201-1 (hardcover, $24.95)
ISBN 0-87816-206-2 (signed hardcover, $39.95)
1. Women cartoonists – United States. 2. Cartooning –
United States – History – 20th century. I. Title.
NC1426.R63   1993
741.5'082-dc20   93-4777
CIP

Credits

TRINA ROBBINS	*author*
DENIS KITCHEN	*publisher*
DAVE SCHREINER	*editor*
RAY FEHRENBACH	*art director*
KEVIN LISON	*design*
CHRISTI SCHOLL	*production*
MICHAEL EASTMAN	
TAMARA SIBERT	
KRISTEN HYLTON	
JAMIE RIEHLE	*marketing*
JIM KITCHEN	*v-p operations*

Acknowledgements

This book would be a very slim volume indeed were it not for all the enthusiastic help given by Bill Blackbeard of the San Francisco Academy of Comic Art. Special thanks are also due to Cole Johnson for the loan of rare and precious comic material reproduced in the first chapter. And more thanks go out (in no particular order) to the following people: Carol Hudzietz Woo, Sally C.B. Lee, Tom Horvitz, Jean Sander, Gary Arlington, Donald Goldsamt, Doug Post, Oz Black, Mike Price, Barb Rausch, Maggie Thompson, Tom Orzechowsky, Arn Saba, David Begin, Chris Nolan, Lee Binswager, Robin Campbell, Heidi MacDonald, and the gang from Copymat.

–T.R.

A CENTURY OF WOMEN CARTOONISTS
Table of Contents

Explanations and Definitions

As the title of this book suggests, this book is about *cartoonists*, and only cartoonists. Women writers are only mentioned when they've worked with a woman cartoonist. If my dear friends who are writers can understand and forgive, so can the readers.

Also, this book is a *history* of women cartoonists. History, as defined by my 1987 *Random House Dictionary of the English Language* is, "a continuous...narrative of past events as relating to a particular people...usually written as a chronological account." While contemporary women cartoonists are included, the chapter dealing with them is merely a sum-up. I have, of course, made every effort to include all contemporary women cartoonists (And if I left you out, it was not intentional. Please accept my apology), but I have not written about any of them in depth. The reader can, and should, find their work easily in comic books, newspapers and books.

In order to keep this book from becoming a lifetime task (which it is, anyway), it was necessary to limit it to women who drew comics, and also to define comics as differing from say, single-panel cartoons. My definition: it's a comic if it includes even one of the following–two or more panels, continuity, or speech balloons inside the panel. In the case of some early comics, the speech was not yet enclosed in balloons, but simply took the form of a line going from the words to the character speaking. In these cases, I stretched my definition a little.

Of Further Interest

FANNY, the Directory of Women Comic Strip Artists, Writers and Cartoonists, directed by Carol Bennett and Cathy Tate, 10 Acklam Road, London W10 5QZ, England. Besides creating the most complete listing of women cartoonists in the world, the remarkable Bennett and Tate publish books of comics by international women cartoonists and mail out a networking newsletter.

European: *AH! NANA,* the only slick magazine collection of comics by women, was published in France from 1976-1979. It included the work of women from all over Europe and the United States. Ironically, in 1992, a woman working with the International Comics Festival at Angouleme, France, wrote: "...It is not always easy to defend [women's issues] in a Latin country. Women's issues are not really an issue here since the '70s." The program for the 1993 comics festival at Angouleme lists no women at all.

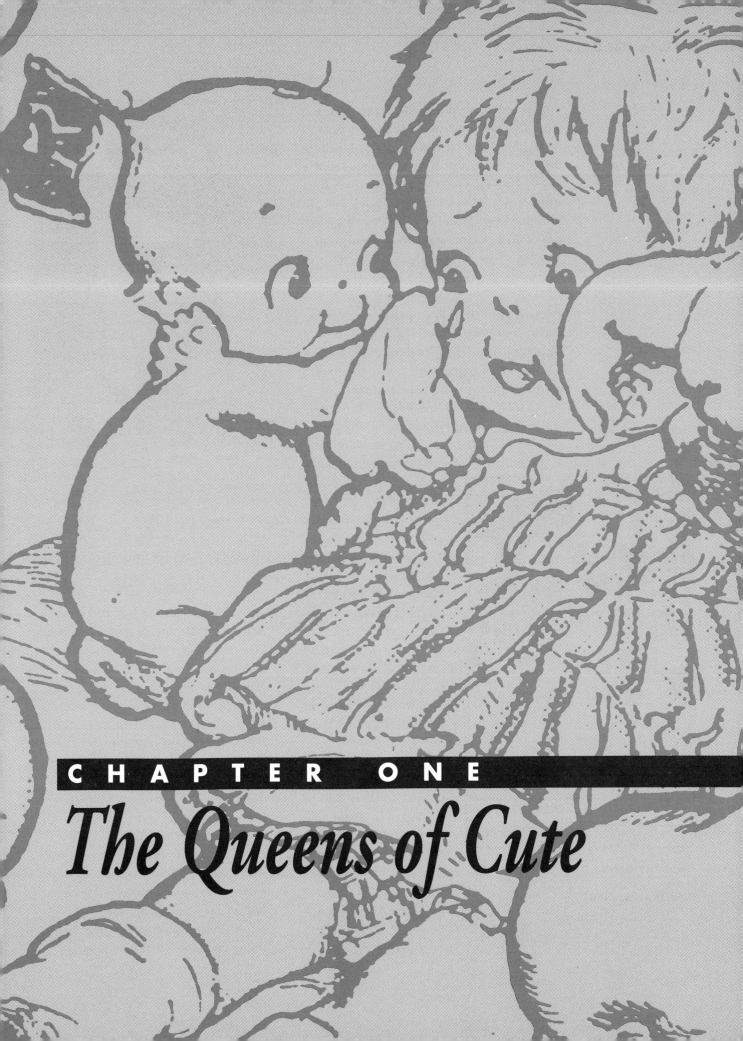

CHAPTER ONE
The Queens of Cute

In 1895, a young illustrator named Rose O'Neill was living with the Sisters of St.Regis at their New York convent, selling illustrations to a host of books and magazines, visiting editors accompanied by a nun. Seven years earlier she had won an art contest sponsored by an Omaha newspaper with a drawing titled "Temptation leading to an abyss." When the judges saw that a 13-year-old girl had won the prize, they made her sit down and produce a drawing on the spot, to prove she was the artist. Two years later she sold her first illustration to *TRUTH* magazine and, at 15, began a career that would span half a century and bring her world fame.

TRUTH magazine seems to have specialized in hiring beginners. At the same time Rose O'Neill was living in a convent, 18-year-old Grace Gebbie sold the magazine her second professional work, a cover drawing of a girl and her cat. The previous year she had drawn place cards of cupids and pretty women, selling them for $2.50 per dozen.

Meanwhile, an 18-year-old Montanan named Fanny Y. Cory was attending the Metropolitan School of Fine Arts in New York City, living with her brother, his wife and her invalid sister. Cory's mother had died of tuberculosis when she was ten. Money was tight, and though Cory was a top student, she didn't stay in school long. Wanting to contribute to her family, the young art student took

Fanny Y. Cory, c.1900

portfolio in hand and approached *Harper's Magazine*.

In her memoirs, hand-written almost three-quarters of a century later on small sheets of lined paper, the artist recalled:

I was walking fast through the Bowery–(a downtown district in New York that had a rather bad reputation) I had my portfolio of pictures under my arm, determined to attempt selling some to Harper's, which was the last of the big publishing houses left down there, the others having gone uptown some years before–I reached the old building–gloomy looking and forbidding– entering I found no elevator so started up the iron stairs so old the steps were worn down the middle.

I trudged up and up–could look down over the railway into the entrance room below–people coming and going–at last on the third floor I found the 'art editors' room—pushed open the door–a young man at the desk greeted me conde-

Drawn by F. Y. CORY.

Trials of a First Baby,
Fanny Y. Cory,
Harper's Bazaar, 1905

scendingly. I said I would like to sell some pictures–he took them and dealt them out like a pack of cards giving them scant attention–asked a question or two–then bundled them back together and handing them back said–'We seldom take beginners' work. If you work hard you may in time hope to place your work here–I advise you to come again when that reputation is made'–I left, mad as hops.

In that year 1895, if any of the three young artists opened up Joseph Pulitzer's New York *World* newspaper, they would have seen a full page color cartoon called "Down in Hogan's Alley," starring a peculiar bald kid in a blue nightshirt. Seven months later, printers experimenting with a new quick-drying yellow ink arbitrarily decided to color the boy's covering bright

Above:
Bun's Puns,
Louise Quarles,
1901

Right:*Woman's Home Companion* **announces the Kewpies, 1910**

yellow. Thus was born what is generally regarded as the first comic strip, R.F. Outcault's *The Yellow Kid.*

By the time the Kid was six years old, comic strips by women had begun to appear on the Sunday pages of America's newspapers. In 1901, Louise Quarles' *Bun's Puns* and Grace Kasson's *Tin Tan Tales for Children* were appearing in the New York *Herald,* and Agnes Repplier lll's *The PhilaBusters* ran in the Philadelphia *Press.*

By that time, Rose O'Neill had divorced her first husband, Gray Latham. A year later, she would marry again, this time to writer Harry Leon Wilson. Their marriage proved productive, with Rose illustrating her husband's books, and writing her own first novel, *The Loves of Edwy,* in 1903. However, by 1908, the couple had parted company. The following year saw the birth of the creatures which were to give Rose immortality– the Kewpies.

According to Rose, these cupid-like creatures came to her in a dream.

1. "Are you the editor of the Scathing Blade?"

2. "Well, I'm the gent you writ about and—"

3. "I jest thought I'd drop in and learn ye—"

4. "Gee, but I wuz scared there for a minute! I thought that fellow was going to stop his subscription.

Above: Some of Rose O'Neill's earliest published work, from *Truth,* 1896.

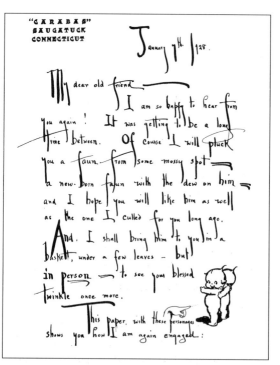

A 1928 letter from Rose O'Neill, embellished with Kewpies.

The Kewpie garter, an ad from *The Ladies' Home Companion,* 1914. Rose O'Neill's creations sold a multitude of goods.

Kewpies appeared from 1909 in the *Ladies' Home Journal, Woman's Home Companion* and *Good Housekeeping,* in the form of one- to three-page stories usually accompanied by verse, a form many of the early comics used. Today, almost a century later, original O'Neill Kewpies sell to collectors for hundreds of dollars, and there still exists an organized Kewpie fandom.

In her personal and professional life, Rose O'Neill often seemed to be two different people. She dressed and looked like a pre-Raphaelite heroine, and was divorced twice in an age when divorce was regarded as a domestic heresy second only to adultery. With her sister, Callista, she held salons attended by most of New York's bohemian crowd at her studio in Greenwich Village; indeed,

Above: Grace Drayton

Below: *Toodles,* Grace Weiderseim, 1903

TOODLES ON THE TRAIN.

Dimples, Grace Drayton, 1917

Aunt Amelia Brings Sallie a Present, But Sallie Didn't Know It

Aunt Amelia—"By jinks, Sallie, I'm glad to get home!"

"Carry that grip carefully, Sallie dear!"

Sallie:—"Oh, sugar! She never gets me anything!"

"I wouldn't have carried her old grip home if I had known that!"

"Oh, Sallie, you dropped the grip! What a shame!"

"I brought you that set of china you admired so much, and now it's all smashed!"

Left: *Sallie Slick,* Jean Mohr, 1902

the song "Rose of Washington Square" was inspired by her. O'Neill was also the creator of a series of drawings which she referred to as "my secret play." This was a more serious experimental work which she kept private; powerful images conjured from dreams and mythology. In 1921 she took this art to Paris for a one-woman show, and was hailed as a reincarnation of Gustave Doré. Along with other souvenirs of the visit, she appears to have brought back a French lover, World War I army officer Jean Gallenné. Journalist Virginia Lynch Maxwell, covering O'Neill's return for the Hearst papers, assumed the couple was married. In the piece entitled "How Cupid Brought the Kewpies Their Ideal Stepfather," Maxwell refused to take seriously O'Neill's some-

what flustered denial:

When the news of her third marriage leaked out, Miss O'Neill denied it with a pretty shake of her curly head.

"It isn't so," she laughed, "I'm still Miss O'Neill."

Which, of course, proved nothing,

Below: *Easy Edgar,* Jean Mohr, 1903

Easy Edgar and the Dog Entertain A Charming Lady.

To make a charming lady laugh—

So she would like him better—

He dressed her doggie up in his new sweater.

Of course his rival came along—

And mixed up with the game.

This is how she treated each. Isn't it a shame?

Above: *The Angel Child,* Kate Carew, 1902

Right: Kate Carew, illustrations for "The Sacred Franchise for Women," 1911

since all the feminine artists of the Village cling to the tradition of their code and flatly refuse to use the prefix "Mrs.," preferring to retain their maiden names.

On the other hand, even before the Kewpies, O'Neill had specialized in producing an artistic combination of adorable children and sentimental verse, making her an outstanding contender for the title "Queen of Cute." Tiny drawings of Kewpies can be found scattered through her personal letters, and her habit of speaking in baby talk is said to have so annoyed her second husband that it contributed to their divorce.

But the uncontested Queen of Cute, Grace Gebbie, was producing *Toodles,* her first strip under her married name of Grace Weidersheim. It set the style for over thirty years of comics by an artist, who, after her second marriage, became known as Grace Drayton. Though the names of the comic strips changed

STRANGE WHAT A DIFFERENCE A MERE MAN MAKES!

Copyright, 1905, by American-Journal-Examiner.

1—Observe the calm indifference of the shop girls toward members of their own sex!   2—And see how attentive they are when a handsome man approaches!

through the years, essentially the same cherubic, apple-cheeked children ran through her comic pages under such titles as *The Strange adventures of Pussy Pumpkin and her Chum Toddles, Dolly Drake and Bobby Blake, The Turr'ble Tales of Kaptin Kiddo, Dolly Dingle, Dolly Dimples*, and *Dottie Darling*. Regarding the last three characters (which also ran as paper doll pages in various magazines), it should be noted that there was a plethora of Dollies, Dotties, Dimples and Darlings in print at the beginning of this century. O'Neill was producing a page for the *Woman's Home Companion* called *Dottie Darling*, Jean Mohr produced a comic strip for the Pulitzer newspapers called *Dolly Dimple*, and in 1913, a male cartoonist named Van Beekman was producing yet another *Dolly Dimple* strip, this one featuring a little girl with a suffragette doll. (To add to the confusion, in the 1920s there was a comic called *Dashing Dot*, drawn by Marge Henderson Buell, who later created *Little Lulu.*)

Jean Mohr, one of the *Dolly Dimple* artists, started in 1902 with an unsettling strip called *Sallie Slick and her Surprising Aunt Amelia*, the story of a pretty girl and her aunt from hell. The *Aunt Amelia* strips were a departure from virtually every

other early comic by women, (and a great many by men) which always featured cute children, either devilish or angelic, and often speaking baby-talk.

Mohr's other strip, *Easy Edgar*, which ran above *Sallie Slick* in the Philadelphia *North American* in 1903, was a more traditional kid strip, although still a bit grotesque, at least by today's standards. The title character, Edgar, in the style of the day, is clad in skirts and petticoats,

Nell Brinkley in 1908

Above: *Strange What a Difference a Difference a Mere Man Makes!*, Marjorie Organ, 1905

Nell Brinkley art from 1908

The helping hand

Why not accept it every time?

Of course you know and enjoy *Campbell's Tomato Soup* as a delicious and nourishing dinner course, but if you use it only now and then on special occasions you don't get half the good of it. Why not enjoy the full benefits of

Campbell's Tomato Soup

When the household cares press hard and heavy —as on wash day, ironing day, house-cleaning days—let this wholesome sustaining food save labor and time for the help, and trouble for you.

Let it simplify your problem on the maid's day out or when you are without a maid. Learn how independent it makes you in unexpected emergencies.

You are never at a loss for a satisfying repast with this tempting soup at hand on the pantry shelf.

It gives added zest to any meal. It is easily prepared in substantial form as the mainstay of a meal in itself. Being already cooked it saves fuel as well as time and labor. And it is readily combined with other simple dishes to make them more inviting and available. In fact, with all its other helpfulness, it helps you to hold down the bills.

How is your supply today?

21 kinds   **10c a can**

WHERE is the woman who doesn't recall the times when she and Belle or Marjory or Nell dressed up in mother's gowns and played housekeeping? Women who are young mothers now will remember serving Jell-O, with all the dressed-up grace displayed by Nan, to a guest with the style put on by Dorothy. It had to be Jell-O, of course, to be the right thing.

JELL-O

There are six pure fruit flavors of Jell-O: Strawberry, Raspberry, Lemon, Orange, Cherry, Chocolate. A new Jell-O Book, just out, is more beautiful and complete than any other ever issued, and it will be sent free to any woman furnishing her name and address.

THE GENESEE PURE FOOD COMPANY
Le Roy, N. Y., and Bridgeburg, Ont.

Top: "Anxious," poem by Margaret G. Hays, illustrated by Grace G. Weiderseim, 1910
Right: Campbell's Soup ad from 1916, Grace Drayton
Above: Jello ad by Rose O'Neill, 1910

and modern readers might assume he was a girl.

Kate Carew's *The Angel Child* also debuted in 1902. (This strip is not to be confused with *Momma's Angel Child*, 1908–1920, by Penny Ross, which despite the name, was by a man.) Carew, sister of *New Yorker* cartoonist Gluyas Williams, exhibited a magnificent disregard for perspective in this strip about the ubiquitous baby-talking little girl in maryjanes, who gets into fresh trouble each day. By 1911, Carew's style had improved greatly, and she was writing and illustrating a page of political commentary and satire for the *New York American*. One of her pages, "The Sacred Right of Franchise for Women = Rubbish!", pokes gentle fun at the anti-suffrage movement, telling of a fictitious interview with "Mrs. Gilbert E. Jones," the society lady leader of an anti-suffrage league. She writes: *...the point is that so long as no woman is allowed to vote there is no danger of Mrs. Gilbert E. Jones's being compelled to vote against her will–she being a woman, although a lady. The league embraces the cream of the ladies who desire not to vote and the cream of the gentlemen who desire not to let them vote, so it's a very harmonious affair.*

In 1902, at the age of 16, Marjorie Organ became the only woman on the art staff of the *New York Journal*, for which she created a number of strips, including *Reggie and the Heavenly Twins* and *Strange What a Difference a Mere Man Makes*. Poor short Reggie, the protagonist of the former strip, was forever trying to win the affections of the two beautiful sisters in the title, only to have them stolen away in the last panel by two equally divine-looking men. The *Mere Man* strip, though beautifully drawn, reflected the direct opposite view of Kate Carew's feminism.

That same year, a 16-year-old student named Nell Brinkley showed her portfolio to the editor of the Denver *Post*, and

THERE are many white soaps, each represented to be just as good as the Ivory; they are not, but like all counterfeits, they lack the peculiar and remarkable qualities of the genuine. Ask for Ivory Soap and insist upon getting it.

The drawing by Fanny Y. Cory, reproduced above, was awarded third prize of Three Hundred Dollars in a recent artists' competition conducted by The Procter & Gamble Co.

Above: Ivory soap ad, Fanny Y. Cory, 1902

Opposite page: *The Turr'ble Tales of Kaptin Kiddo*, Margaret Hays and Grace Weiderseim, 1910

GRETCHEN GRATZ AND HER FRIENDS DISCOVER A BEEHIVE

Said Gretchen Gratz to Hans and Claus:
"Please hold this rope whilst I
Jump over it; I jump real well,
But don't you hold it high."

"All right," said Hans, "Here, Claus, take hold
And don't you let it go,
We'll hold it up about two feet,
She'll soon·jump that I know."

Now naughty Claus held up his end,
And as she missed, he said;
"Oh, you can't jump a little bit,
Let me get there instead."

"Now, I will jump three feet or more
As sure as I'm alive."
He did it sure enough, but bumped
Right in a big bee hive.

The bees were very much annoyed
At being thus put out;
They swarmed around those children three,
And made them run and shout!

Now Hans and Gretchen got away
But Claus got left behind,
And a place on him that was not stung
It will be hard to find!

Above: Gretchen Gratz, Inez Townsend, 1904

Right: Snooks and Snicks, Inez Tribit, 1913

SNOOKS AND SNICKS PLAYED HOOKEY

"Now, children," said their mother, "don't
Be late for school today.
It's very nearly 9, so please
Don't loiter by the way."

"Oh, how I hate to go to school,"
Said Snicks. "Let's run away!"
"All right!" cried Snooks. "That suits me fine!
No school for me today!"

So little Sue went on alone.
She did not see them go.
Said Snooks: "Let's sit beneath that tree—
We'll have some fun, I know."

Now when the children were in school
Their teacher to them said:
"We won't any school today,
But have a treat instead."

She took them out into the woods
And had a lovely treat.
"Today's my birthday, children dear;
Take all you want to eat!"

On her way home Sue met the twins
And told them of the spread.
"You bad boys, you'd have had some if
You'd gone to school instead!"

was hired as an illustrator for $7 a week. Within a year, she had moved to the Denver *Times,* and, four years later she came to New York to work for Hearst at his *Journal.* In 1907 she was illustrating the Harry K. Thaw murder trial. Thaw stood accused of killing famed architect Stanford White over the affections of beautiful Evelyn Nesbitt, Thaw's wife and White's ex-lover. Nesbitt, who had modeled for Charles Dana Gibson, was a perfect candidate for Brinkley's pen. The glamorous "Brinkley girls," with their floating masses of curls, ruffles and laces, would thrill a generation of women throughout the 1920s, and inspire future cartoonists such as Hilda Terry, Marty Links, Selby Kelly, and especially Dale Messick, who created *Brenda Starr.*

In 1902 Fanny Y. Cory, by then a successful illustrator, moved back to Montana. Two years later she married childhood friend Fred Cooney and settled at his ranch near the tiny com-

JENNIE AND JACK, ALSO THE LITTLE DOG JAP

munity of Canyon Ferry. Living in what was still the wild West, she continued to work, illustrating six books between 1905 and 1913. Cooney would take her packaged art on horseback to the post office. Gradually, however, Cory's art became secondary to raising a family, and it wasn't until the 1920s that she returned to her art, this time in the form of comics.

In 1905 Grace Drayton, still working under the name Weiderseim, drew a strip written by her sister, Margaret Gebbie Hays: *The Adventures of Dolly Drake and Bobby Blake in Storyland*. She would work with her sister again in 1909, with Margaret writing and Grace drawing *The Turb'le Tales of Kaptin Kiddo*. The sisters also collaborated for publications such as *Youth's Companion*, where Grace would illustrate short poems by Margaret. In the same year, between the numerous comics, magazine illustrations, paper dolls and children's books she was turning out,

Grace Drayton managed to create the Campbell Kids. The Campbell Soup Co. could not have asked for a better image, since *every* cherubic child drawn by Drayton looked like the Campbell Kids. (Neither O'Neill nor Cory is likely to have resented Drayton's prize account, since O'Neill was at that time drawing all the Jello ads, and Cory was working for Ivory Soap.)

Margaret Gebbie Hays attempted a strip of her own in 1908, both writing and drawing *Jennie and Jack, Also the Little Dog Jap*. The influence of her sister's style is evident. Although *Jennie and Jack* is no worse than many of the mediocre strips that ran at the time, it's obvious that Margaret did not possess her sister's artistic talent.

A popular convention was drawing children in fashions of the previous century. Illustrations of this sort can be found in old *Mother Goose* books, and children's

Above: *Jennie and Jack, Also the Little Dog Jap,* Margaret G. Hays

FLORA FLIRTS WITH A CHARMING SANTA CLAUS

Miss Flora Flirt feels out of sight
At a party gay on Christmas night.

Old Santa Claus, midst jollity,
Takes the presents off the tree.

When he brings Flo a present fine,
She flirts with him with eyes that shine.

She leads him 'neath the mistletoe—
And then, of course, he kisses Flo.

By the punchbowl their action's most a "scandal"—
But he leans too close to a lighted candle

Flora Flirt,
Katherine Price, 1913

Poor Flora shrieks—his beard's aflame.
Which spoils their little flirting game.
The Moral—On Christmas, 'neath the mistletoe
is the "safest" place to keep **a beau**.

KATE AND KARL MAKE A SHOW OF PARTY MANNERS

books by Johnny Gruelle and others. Inez Townsend used the style when she drew *Gretchen Gratz* in 1904 and 1905, and later in 1913 when, now signing her work Inez Tribit, she produced *Snooks and Snicks, the Mischievous Twins.* The stories follow a familiar pattern: adorable children get into trouble. Indeed, kids mixing it up with beehives seems to have been a convention; we can see examples of it in *Gretchen Gratz* and Margaret Hays' *Jennie and Jack.*

Another strip that featured old-fashioned children was Mary A. Hays' *Kate and Karl, the Cranford Kids,* from 1911 and 1912. The use of the name Cranford is an in-joke. Fred Crane, editor of the Philadelphia *North American*'s comic syndicate, published Mary Hays as well as Jean Mohr, Inez Tribit, Grace Drayton and Katherine Price (who drew *Flora Flirt*

in 1913). Crane, who probably printed more women cartoonists than anyone else, came from Cranford, New Jersey, a town founded in colonial days by his ancestors.

When looking at Mary A. Hays' comics, one is struck by the art's resemblance to Grace Drayton's style, a resemblance that provoked at least one collector to speculate that Mary A. Hays and Margaret Gebbie Hays were the same person. However, in a bit of sleuthing worthy of V.I. Warshawsky, Lorraine Burdick, in the 1974 *Celebrity Doll Journal*, determined the connection. On a paper doll page drawn by Grace Drayton in 1928 for *Woman's World*, Drayton had written, "Dear Children, I have a little grandniece Peggy Anne Huber. She is also my godchild." Then Burdick found a 1919 *Delineator* page containing Mary A. Hays

Above: *Kate and Karl, the Cranford Kids,* Mary A. Hays, 1917

Tessie Is a Tomboy! Tomboy! Tomboy!

Above: *Tessie is a Tomboy,* Eliza Curtis,1910. The author knows nothing about the creator of this delightful strip, and so simply presents it for your enjoyment.

art, but signed Mary Hays Huber. Burdick writes, "Back-tracking from grandniece Peggy Anne Huber leads to niece Mary Hays Huber; Mary A. Hays leads to sister Margaret Gebbie Hays. This means that Margaret must have been some five to 10 years older than Grace for Mary to be old enough to be drawing well in 1911 (the earliest known artwork by Mary Hays)." Burdick also points out a page of Drayton's paper dolls from the year that

Mary Hays changed her name to Huber, in which Dolly Dingle is a flower girl at her aunt's wedding, "perhaps a carry-over from real life."

Until someone else comes up with evidence to refute Lorraine Burdick's conclusions, I think it can be assumed that Grace Gebbie Drayton, Margaret Gebbie Hays and Mary A. Hays represent two generations of woman cartoonists—a case of sisterhood being powerful.

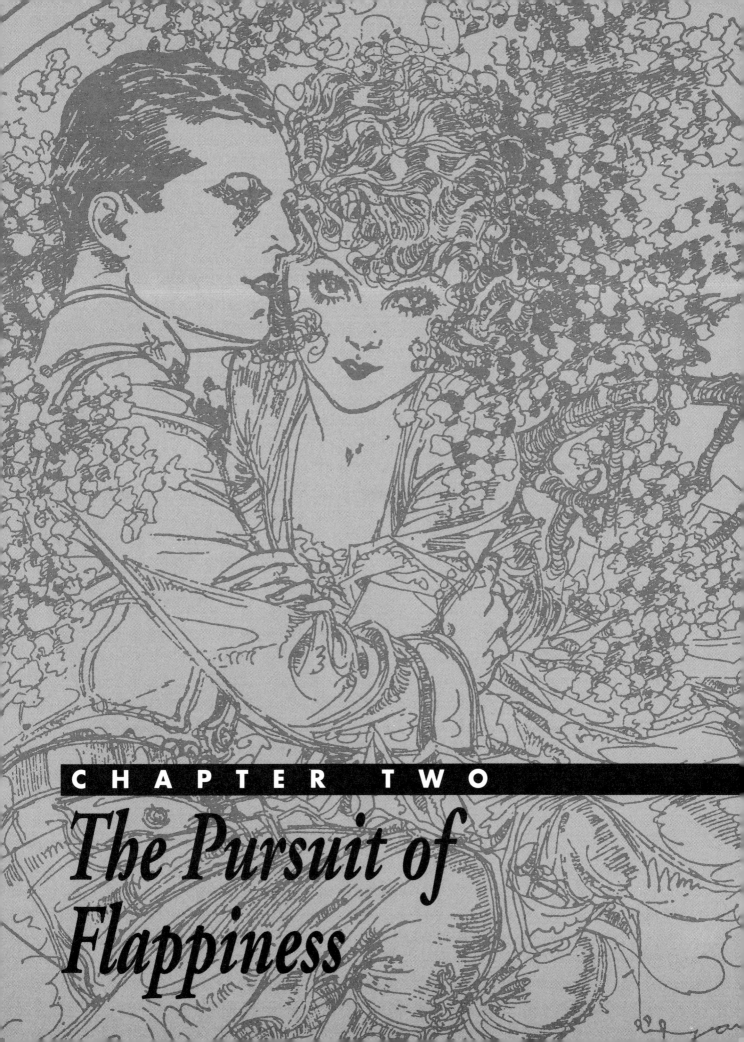

CHAPTER TWO
The Pursuit of Flappiness

At the 1992 opening of a women cartoonists show at the San Francisco Cartoon Art Museum, attendees watched in awe as guest of honor Dale Messick, creator of *Brenda Starr,* strolled through the exhibit. The 86-year-old dean of women cartoonists paused before a page by Nell Brinkley, and her eyes shone like the starry orbs of her creation as she studied the delicate pen work on the ruffles, lace and windblown hair of the elegantly drawn "Brinkley Girl." Brinkley had been Messick's greatest influence.

If one person can be said to have set the style for the majority of women cartoonists during the 1920s, that person was Nell Brinkley. As early as 1908, the glamorous creatures she created were inspiring controversy and fan mail. After a critical letter asking, "Is there any good reason why a woman's head should be portrayed as weather-beaten moss instead of human hair?", the Los Angeles *Examiner* felt compelled to defend their young star artist by stating that Brinkley herself possessed the kind of hair she drew: "Miss Brinkley pictures chiefly hair, which a reader sacreligeously calls 'moss', and Miss Brinkley, curiously enough, at the first superficial glance, is chiefly hair—certainly she wears not less than a bushel of the very lightest, curliest kind." The article went on to compare her art to Raphael, Michaelangelo, Boucher, Titian, Botticelli and Da Vinci.

Another issue of the *Examiner* printed tributes to the Brinkley Girl from readers, some of whom were moved to verse. W. L. Larned wrote:

The sweetest, neatest, fleetest maid—the leader in her class,
Give me the stylish, smilish, wilish, dashing Brinkley Lass.

Another poet who signed herself "A Young Woman Who Admires Her Work," wrote:

Nell Brinkley, creator of The Call and Post's "Brinkley Girl," who is in San Francisco marveling at the beauty of San Francisco girls.

PHOTO BY INTERNATIONAL NEWS SERVICE

Nell Brinkley, photo from the San Francisco *Call,* 1915

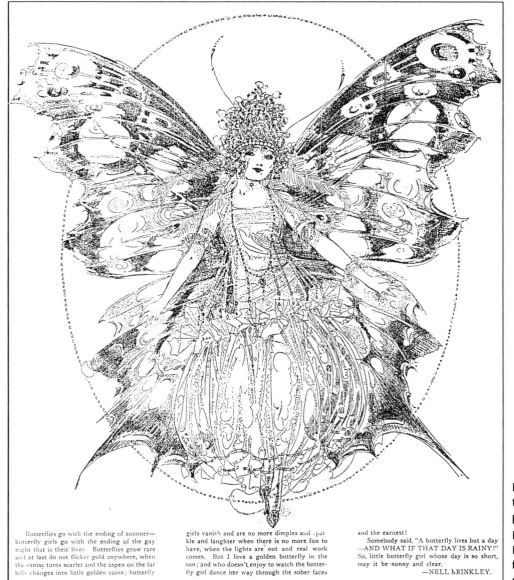

Butterflies go with the ending of summer—butterfly girls go with the ending of the gay night that is their lives. Butterflies grow rare and at last do not flicker gold anywhere, when the sumac turns scarlet and the aspen on the far hills changes into little golden coins; butterfly girls vanish and are no more dimples and spar kle and laughter when there is no more fun to have, when the lights are out and real work comes. But I love a golden butterfly in the sun; and who doesn't enjoy to watch the butter fly girl dance her way through the sober faces and the earnest!

Somebody said, "A butterfly lives but a day —AND WHAT IF THAT DAY IS RAINY!" So, little butterfly girl whose day is so short, may it be sunny and clear.
—NELL BRINKLEY.

Left: A closer look at the art in the newspaper photo

Below: The New Nell Brinkley Bob Curler, from a catalogue, circa 1920

You are spritely and you're tinkley,
You seem just on the Brink-ley
Of putting all the others in the shade;
So blessings on you, girlie,
With the pen so whirley-twirley,
May your newspaper shadow never fade!

Florenz Zeigfeld, the showman who made his fortune "glorifying the American girl" on stage, featured in his Follies a Brinkley Girl, one of whom was the future silent film star May Murray. And by the '20s, female Brinkley fans who aspired to the clouds of curls worn by the heroines of such strips as *The Fortunes of Flossie, Romances of Gloriette,* or *The Adventures of Prudence Prim,* could choose between Nell Brinkley Hair Wavers or The New Nell

Brinkley Bob Curler, at 9¢ per card.

Brinkley herself appears to have lived quietly and conservatively. Unlike Rose O'Neill and Grace Drayton, she stayed married to one man all her life, was a Presbyterian, and supported the Republican Party. Brinkley continued working well into the 1930s, and although her later style became more simplified, it never lost the characteristic elegance which personified the Brinkley Girl. She retired in 1937, at 51, although she continued to illustrate books and occa-

The Adventures of Prudence Prim, Nell Brinkley, 1925

The Fortunes of Flossy, Nell Brinkley, 1927

Kitty Courageous   THE ADVENTURES OF A TOMBOY   By STELLA FLORES

Copyright, 1914, by International News Service

"If you want some fun, Miss Kitty," grinned Broncho Pete, "jump on a gentle hoss, and ride over to see me break the 'Demon.'" | Kitty picked out a little horse with a mild face, saying, "I think I can ride you without a saddle." But the minute she was on he reared . | The horse leaped, bucked and whirled, and Kitty felt like the map of Europe. "If any one asked my opinion, I should say this animal would make a very good pinwheel, but I'm still on deck," she chuckled. | "Excuse my delay," she called to Broncho Pete, as she rode up. "I'm ready to watch you break the 'Demon.'" "Jumping Jehosophat!" yelled Pete, "that's the 'Demon' your're on! You didn't know it, but he's the fellow."

sionally draw for magazines.

Coincidentally, both Rose O'Neill and Nell Brinkley died in 1944. An obituary commented on Brinkley's great influence and compared her to O'Neill: "The late Nell Brinkley attracted more amateur copyists than did Charles Dana Gibson. Like Rose O'Neill, who came before her, she was quite an eyeful herself, and was past master as a cheesecake artist."

By the end of the 1920s and well into the 1930s, a score of talented women, following in Brinkley's satin-shod footsteps, were turning out comics featuring chic and clever flappers. Probably the most famous of these was the multi-talented Ethel Hays, creator of comics, single panel cartoons, paper doll books, children's book illustrations, and full color Sunday pages. The Sunday pages, while similar to and obviously inspired by those of Brinkley, were done in Hays' cleaner, more art deco style. In a newspaper interview from 1927, Hays admitted a strong John Held, Jr. influence: "I adore John Held, Jr … when I was battling with my first drawings in the newspaper office I had to keep his drawings out of sight; his influence was so strong that I was prone to imitate."

Her favorite woman artist, she said, was Brinkley: "Her work is exquisite."

Brought up in Billings, Montana, Ethel Hays studied art at the Los Angeles School of

Top: *Kitty Courageous,* Stella Flores. As early as 1914, Nell Brinkley was already influencing women cartoonists like Stella Flores of the San Francisco *Call and Post.*

Above: Silent screen star May Murray, "The Radiant Nell Brinkley Girl of the Follies," from *Theater Magazine,* 1920.

Right: Rose O'Neill, posing with a Kewpie in her later years.

THE SITTING ROOM WHERE INFORMAL TEAS ARE GIVEN   WASHINGTON D.C

Above: In 1934, shortly before her retirement, Nell Brinkley gives the glamour treatment to Eleanor Roosevelt.

Left: Paper dolls by Nell Brinkley, 1928. Like her predecessors Rose O'Neill and Grace Drayton, Brinkley drew paper dolls. Throughout the history of comics, women have added paper dolls to their comics.

Ethel Hays Sunday page, 1931

ETHEL: April Showers Did All This

BUDDING SEASON
THE DAY OF THE DEBUTANTE

THE HEAD BOUQUET

THE WRIST BOUQUET

THE GOOD OLD CORSAGE

THE WAY THE FLORIST WOULD HAVE HER

THE SHOULDER BOUQUET

THE OLD-FASHIONED ARM BOUQUET

AND

THE NEW ANKLE BOUQUET

Above: *April Showers Did All This*, Ethel Hays, 1925

Right: *Metamorphosis*, Ethel Hays, 1926

Art and Design and the Art League in New York. After the United States entered World War I, she taught art to disabled soldiers at government hospitals in Washington, Colorado, Tennessee and Ohio, meanwhile taking a correspondence course in drawing herself. The director of her school showed her work to the editor of the Cleveland *Press*, who immediately called Hays and hired her. A 1928 newspaper article described the artist's work on *Vic and Ethel*, the feature she drew: "She and a girl reporter did a picture feature stunt every day ... They climbed church steeples and went down in diving suits. They rode speed boats and broke ice in the lake in order to go in swimming. Ethel's girl drawings were a city fixture."

The article went on to describe her as "a real feather in the feminist's cap..."

Within a year Hays had become a nationally syndicated cartoonist. Her first syndicated strip, aptly named *Ethel*, consisted of satire

ETHEL: Metamorphosis

A COMPOSITE PICTURE OF THE WAY ALL THE CO-EDS LOOK TO THE CYNICAL MALE STUDENT ~

— AND THE WAY THEY ALL LOOK TO HIM AFTER HE HAS FALLEN IN LOVE WITH ONE OF THEM

Top: *Gay and Her Gang,* Gladys Parker, 1926. "Life, liberty, and the pursuit of flappiness." Those familiar with Parker's later style would never recognize this strip as hers, if not for the signature.

Above: *Gay and Her Gang,* about 1927. Approximately a year after starting her strip, Gladys Parker developed her own recognizable style. She signs her name the same way that she would sign it 20 years later in *Mopsy.*

Left: A Lux soap ad by Gladys Parker, circa 1930.

and social commentary. *Flapper Fanny,* a single panel cartoon followed soon after, and by 1928 she was producing Sunday pages.

Hays had gotten married in 1924 and soon after started a family. By the time she gave birth to her second daughter, the artist's workload had simply become too heavy. Rather than lavishly illustrated Sunday color pages, Hays passed *Flapper Fanny* on to Gladys Parker, who had previously drawn a sophisticated flapper strip called *Gay and Her Gang.* The dry wit in *Gay and Her Gang* often reminds the reader of another Parker, Dorothy. When a character talks about her rights to "life, liberty and the pursuit of flappiness," she seems to speak for all the strips of that decade which featured stylish, wise-crack-

FLAPPER FANNY says Nelly declara...

It isn't long before the first blush of youth is succeeded by the second blush of the drug store.

—Por regla general, en toda exposición de vestidos, la que más aceptación tiene es la que menos lo lleva.

NELLY Y BETTY,

—Vamos, dime qué te ha pasado. ¿Por qué lloras?
—¡Porque sería la chica más popular de la clase, si tuviera tres hermanos!

—Voy a mandar este pull-over por correo. ¿Por cuánto tendré que asegurarlo? Mi hermana dice que no tejería otro ni por un millón.

Flapper Fanny by (left to right) Ethel Hays, Gladys Parker, Sylvia. The last two strips are from a Spanish magazine, where *Flapper Fanny* was reprinted under the name *Nelly*.

ing young women.

Under Gladys Parker, the single panel strip took on a cartoonier style, and its flapper protagonist grew to closely resemble her delineator, one of several cases where a woman drew herself as the heroine of her own strip. During this time, Parker was also drawing a series of comic strip ads for Lux soap.

By the late 1930s, Parker had moved to a better paying syndicate, where she created the long lasting character, *Mopsy*. *Flapper Fanny*

Marianne, Ethel Hays, mid-1930s

Above: *Marianne,* Virginia Krausman, late 1930s. The top strip was drawn right after Krausman took over from Ethel Hays, and Krausman is imitating her style. The bottom strip, drawn a year later, shows the artist working in her own, more realistic style.

Below: *Gentlemen Prefer Blondes,* 1926. Virginia Huget's first strip. The artist still has much to learn about panel borders.

Babs in Society, Virginia Huget, 1927

Above: Virginia Clark Hudzietz/Huget and Coon Williams Hudzietz, mid-1920s.

Right: Virginia Huget's flapper hula girl from *Miss Alladin,* 1929.

was taken over by a cartoonist known only by her first name, Sylvia. Sylvia added a kid sister to the panel and continued it into the 1940s. Meanwhile, Ethel Hays, who obviously couldn't stop, drew one last flapper strip in 1936, *Marianne.* Virginia Krausman drew the strip after Hays left, copying Hays' style at first, but soon giving it a more detailed, though still stylishly deco, look. Hays went on to a long career illustrating children's books and paper dolls, both of which presumably paid more than her comics.

Another remarkably talented and prolific creator was Virginia Huget, who during the later '20s and early '30s seemed to produce a new strip every year. Born Virginia Clark in Dallas, Texas in 1900, she married her childhood sweetheart, Coon Williams Hudzietz, and moved to Chicago, where she attended the Art Institute. The name Hudzietz was pronounced Huget, so in 1926, when the artist sold her first strip, *Gentlemen Prefer Blondes,* to the Bell syndicate, it was natural that she signed it not with a suspiciously "foreign" name that was difficult to pronounce, but with the more glamorous "French-sounding" Huget.

By 1927, Huget was drawing *Babs In Society,* a full

Virginia Huget strips. Top: *Campus Capers.* Bottom: *Molly the Manicure Girl.* Same characters, different stories.

PEGGY LUX IN SYLMANIA—Her Fashion Show

Above: Virginia Huget, Lux soap ad, 1932

Below: *Skippy*, 1937. The son of Virginia Clark Hudzietz/Huget remembers seeing this strip on his mother's drawing table when she "ghosted" for Percy Crosby.

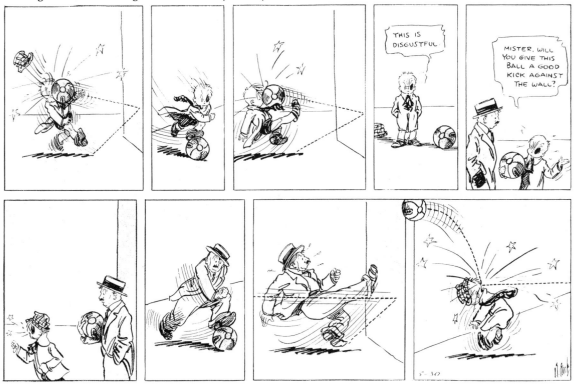

By DODO

DODO AND DOT SEEK THE SOCIAL LIFE
Everybody Spreads Himself in Peacock Alley

Dodo and Dot, Dot Cochran, early twenties. The little figure in the top left hand corner is a self-portrait of the artist.

page Sunday color strip that chronicled the adventures of a spunky little flapper working in a department store, who inherits a fortune from her long-lost uncle Ebenezer. In 1928 the artist drew *Campus Capers,* a daily-sized flapper strip, and *Flora's Fling,* a colored

Sunday page. In 1929 she did another Sunday page, *Miss Aladdin,* which is Huget at her best, sprightly and very deco. In *Babs,* the artist, obviously still under the influence of Ethel Hays, gave her heroine a dark curly *Flapper Fanny* hairdo. *Miss Aladdin* sports a blonde

ME AND MY BOY FRIEND   *The Worm Turns*

Me and My Boyfriend, Dot Cochran, 1925

Annibelle, Dorothy Urfer, 1931

Annibelle, Virginia Krausman, 1936

DASHING DOT
Finds the way
to a man's heart

"O, mama!" cried Dot, "I'm going to invite
Dear Dickie for dinner on Saturday night.
He likes me a lot, of that I am sure,
But thinks that my cooking is terribly poor."

"Now you and dear Dad run along, and I'll do
The cooking for us—just a dinner for two.
I'm sure that I can convince him, and soon
Wedding bells you will hear and the Mendelssohn tune."

So Mother and Father arranged to go out.
And, O! how Dot hustled and bustled about!
A soup and a meat pie, a salad, a cake—
There were all kinds of things that our Dotty could make.

The cook book she read with the greatest of care;
Why, it really took no time at all to prepare
A dainty and truly choice little repast.
Thank goodness! 'Twas all in the oven at last!

The table looked lovely, and dear gallant Dick
Declared it made restaurants look very sick.
Till Dot, at the oven, threw it open— O my!
What a queer looking cake and funny meat pie!

"I did what the cook book said," wailed weeping Dot.
"That horrid old range must have been very hot."
Dick bade her cheer up. "Never mind, Dotty dear,
We'll never be hungry as long as I'm here!"

"For as a Boy Scout I could rustle a meal
That I have to admit had distinctive appeal.
I can't bake a cake, nor can I roast meat;
But, really, my flapjacks are quite hard to beat."

So quickly they mixed in the bowl a big batter
And played pat-a-cake with the merriest chatter.
"Why worry, my dear, this dough is the money;
And you, angel child, are forever my honey!"

Verses and Sketches
BY "MARGE"

Dashing Dot, Marge Henderson, 1929

Two strips by Fay King, early thirties.

Louise Brooks bob, and Huget's rendering of this quintessential flapper as a hula girl is unforgettable. The heroine of *Molly the Manicure Girl*, a daily strip done that same year, also has a Louise Brooks haircut, and looks exactly like the heroine of Huget's previous strip, *Campus Capers*. Huget appears to have done a series of these strips, all in the mode of *Gentlemen Prefer Blondes*, featuring two young women, a blonde and a Louise Brooks lookalike brunette. Like Gladys Parker, Huget somehow found the time to draw Lux soap ads, which won a first prize from the Art Directors League of New York.

In 1936, her style subtly changing with the fashions of the times, she drew *Dizzie Dolly Ditties*. She seemed to possess the ability to change her style as needed, and was so proficient at mimicking other styles that she sometimes substituted for other artists. In 1937, during a time when Percy Crosby, creator of the popular strip *Skippy,* went through a period of alcoholism so severe that he could not meet his deadlines, she carried it on under his name. Her imitation of Crosby's style is flawless. By 1944, under her maiden name of Virginia Clark, she had taken over *Oh Diana!* from artist Don Flowers, and was rendering it

beautifully in his style.

Dot Cochran was born in Toledo, Ohio in 1901. Her father, Negley Cochran, was editor and publisher of the *Toledo Bee;* one brother was a cartoonist and her sister and other brothers were journalists. Later, she became the aunt of Martha Blanchard, whose single panel cartoons appeared in such magazines as *Collier's* and *The Saturday Evening Post*, and sister-in-law to Frederick Opper, creator of *Alphonse and Gaston* and *Happy Hooligan*. With a family like that, it seems natural that while still in her early twenties she should have sold her first feature, *Dot and Dodo*. As with Hays' *Vic and Ethel*, the young Cochran illustrated the adventures of herself and Dodo, the writer. When Cochran sold her charming flapper strip, *Me and My Boyfriend*, she chose the Hearst chain's King Features Syndicate. rather than the *Bee's* Scripps-Howard Syndicate, so no one could accuse her of using her father's influence. *Me and My Boyfriend* lasted only until 1927, when Cochran married and moved to England, where she illustrated several books.

Joining the flapper party in 1933 was the strip *Annibelle* drawn by Dorothy Urfer, and taken over in 1936 by Virginia Krausman, who

Fay King's tribute to pioneer aviator Beryl Markham.

seemed to specialize in taking over other women's strips.

Marjorie Henderson, who was to gain fame in 1934 as the creator of the immortal *Little Lulu*, was 25 years old in 1929 when she wrote and drew *Dashing Dot*. Her familiar *Little Lulu* style is recognizable in this flapper strip, combined with the obvious influence of John Held, Jr. The strip is signed simply, Marge, the same way she later signed her *Saturday Evening Post* cartoons.

Fay King, a top cartoonist for over two decades, was referred to by Chuck Thorndike in his 1939 book, *The Business of Cartooning*, as one of the top five women cartoonists in America. Her work was an exception to the pretty girl flapper strips drawn by women in the '20s and '30s. While drawing other characters in a breezy, stylish manner, King put herself into the strips, and drew herself as looking like Olive Oyl. With herself as the main character, King's strips consisted of personal opinions, and included her personal life. Newspapers covered her marriage to world Lightweight Boxing champion Oscar Matthew "Battling" Nelson in 1913, and also covered their colorful divorce. A 1916 article reports:

> The "Durable Dane," as Nelson is known professionally, charges that Mrs. Nelson never loved him, but regarded him

merely as a "li'l pal"...letters by Mrs. Nelson,...referring to the ex- champion as a "Dear little woolly lamb," admitted she never loved him, but was "very grateful—that's all."

In a 1918 cartoon, King draws a man labeled "My 'Fay'-vorite Pest," saying to her, "You married Battling Nelson, didn't you! He sure waz a great little scrapper...", while the scrawny, big-footed Fay caricature replies, "SAY—I'm tryin to live that down!"

The Battling Nelson episode was the occasion for King to meet journalist Gene Fowler, sent to interview her for his newspaper. The two became friends, and his memoirs give us an excellent description of the artist:

> I was unprepared to come upon so much vitality in such a small package...I observed that she was dark-complexioned with very large dark eyes, and that she wore numerous pieces of jewelry which chimed like bells...There were gold hoops in her ears, and on one forefinger she wore a heavy gold band to which was affixed a cartoon effigy of herself... she liked gay colors also and when she had assembled her various scarves and sashes, she reminded me of the mountain flowers of August.

CHAPTER THREE

Depression Babies and Babes

The frenetic party that was the Roaring Twenties crashed to a close in 1929, bringing with it the slow fade of the flapper strip, although some of them hung on through the '30s. The average heroine of these strips had been a pretty girl, often a co-ed, with nothing on her mind but boys. But now America, plunged into the Great Depression, tossed aside the frivolity of the '20s in favor of a new kind of comic: the Depression strip.

Echoing the new mood of the times, this type of strip featured unglamorous protagonists dealing with real problems: poor but happy American households; upbeat, unflappable orphans; plucky working girls out to earn a living rather than merely have a good time.

Martha Orr's *Apple Mary* can be considered the quintessential Depression strip. The stories revolved around old Mary, who sold apples on a street corner, and her friends and family, all of them as big-hearted as they were poor. After drawing *Mary* for seven years, Orr, who had gotten married, retired to raise a family, and the strip was taken over by her talented assistant, Dale Conner. She changed the name to *Mary Worth's Family* and signed it simply "Dale." Soon Conner acquired a writer, Allen Saunders, at which time she started signing the strip with a combination of their two names, Dale Allen. Unhappy with the direction her strip was taking under Saunders, Conner eventually left it to team with her husband, also a comic writer. Unfortunately, none of their projects panned out. Saunders found Ken Ernst to draw the art, and *Mary Worth*, in much changed form, survives today (although

MARY WORTH'S FAMILY

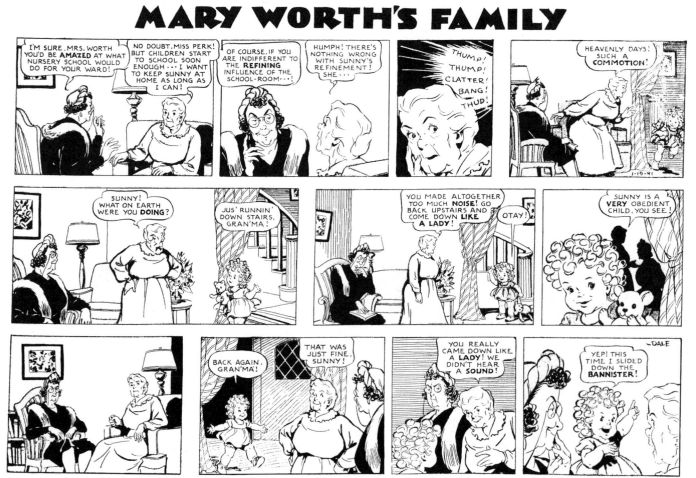

Mary Worth's Family, Dale Conner, 1941

DIZZY DOLLY DITTIES
by Virginia Huget

Gallantry, where art thou hid
In this age of shove and skid?

SUNDAY, DECEMBER 13, 1936.

Trade Mark Registration Applied For

1.

In the days of Good Queen Bess
Courtiers showed a rare finesse—
Uncle Walter Raleigh's cloak
Saved Her Nibs from
   many a soak.

2.

In this time of Edward Eight
Chivalry's gone out of date;
Snooty roadsters spot and splash us
When their drivers fail to mash us.

3.

In the reign of Good Queen Anne
Debs all rated a sedan
Borne by linkmen hale and hearty
To each whist or sherry party.

4.

Though your beauty ties The Follies
You don't rate a seat in trolleys;
You must take it on the shins or
Lump it, under Edward Windsor!

Dizzy Dolly Ditties, Virginia Huget, December, 1936. By 1936, Huget's carefree flappers of the twenties had become harried working girls, splashed by rich folks' cars and struggling for a seat on the trolley.

Apple Mary, Martha Orr, 1939

and I went to her and had better success than with the young man in the Bowery — in fact I was soon making most of my living through that publication — "Trials of a first baby" "Trials of a small boy" and many others — also found favor with "Youth's Companion" and still worked steadly for Saint Nicholas and Century —

I was walking down a long hall of the Century building when the President of that Company caught up with me and put a Fatherly arm accross my shoulders — calling me "The little sister of the Century Co." I was much pleased you may be sure —

Once as I was going in to buy a ticket to see "Maud Adams" in "Peter Pan" I heard a girl whisper close to me. "That's her, that's Maud Adams"? I looked around to see where she looked and she was pointing at me — As Maud Adams was not a pretty

A page from Fanny Y. Cory's unpublished memoirs, hand written on lined paper towards the end of her life. Here the artist writes about her beginnings as an illustrator.

The Mexican Way, editorial cartoon, from the Columbus *Monitor,* Edwina Dumm, 1916

under other hands).

Another homey little American household consisted of a boy, his dog, and his granny. Edwina Dumm's *Cap Stubbs and Tippy* was at its peak of popularity during the Depression, although it had been running since 1918. In 1916, Edwina Dumm started her career in the Columbus *Monitor,* as possibly America's first female political cartoonist. By the following year she was drawing a humor page, *Spot-light Sketches.* The page consisted mostly of single panel cartoons, and had a strip running on the bottom entitled *The Meanderings Of Minnie,* always

subtitled "passed by the board of censors," starring a little girl and her fluffy dog. *Minnie* must have been the most popular item on the page, because soon it was running on its own. When Dumm became nationally syndicated in 1918, Minnie underwent a sex change, the dog became a shorthair, and the artist began signing her work with just her first name, Edwina, a practice she continued for the run of the strip. In the early 1930s, Dumm was given a little long-haired dog, and Tippy became a longhair again, and stayed that way for the next 30 years. *Cap Stubbs and Tippy* ran until 1960, and

Spotlight Sketches, humor page from the Columbus *Monitor,* Edwina Dumm, 1917

"Cap" Stubbs, an early version of *Cap Stubbs and Tippie,* Edwina Dumm, 1920

Tippie, in his final form, Edwina Dumm, 1941

Edwina Dumm herself lived to be 95 years old, owning a succession of cute little longhaired dogs.

While *Tippy* is considered the first continuity strip by a woman, and *Apple Mary* the first dramatic continuity strip by a woman, the award for first action continuity must go to a now-forgotten artist named Caroline M. Sexton. In 1934, signing her work "C.M. Sexton," she pro-

duced *Luke and Duke,* a strip that took place during the First World War. The adventures of two American doughboys and Yvonne, the beautiful Belgian orphan they somehow acquire, is drawn in a style reminiscent of Belgian cartoonist Herge's comic, *Tintin,* and also at times seems like an early version of Bill Mauldin's World War II cartoon, *Up Front.* It's understandable why Sexton would use her initials

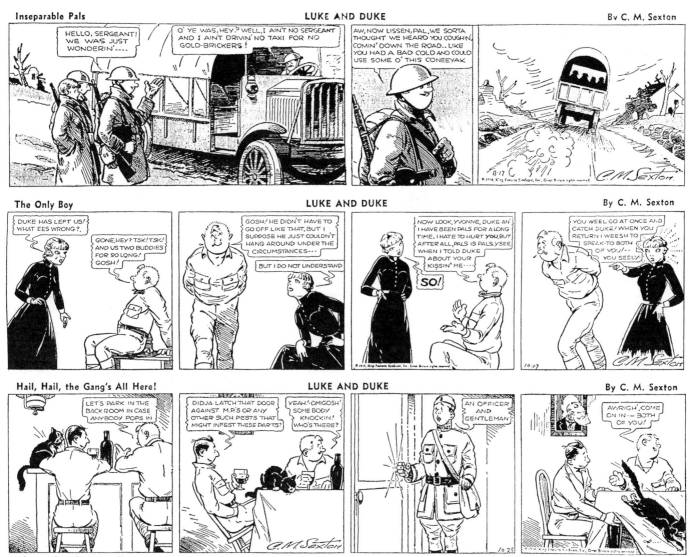

Luke and Duke, Caroline M. Sexton, 1934

rather than her full name for this charming, but definitely male-oriented strip.

Meanwhile the original major women cartoonists from the beginning of the century had by no means retired. Rose O'Neill's *Kewpie* strips were running in newspapers across the nation. She would continue to draw Kewpies until her death in 1944.

O'Neill's contemporary, Fanny Y. Cory, who, like too many other women of the time, put aside her career to raise a family on the Montana ranch where she and her husband lived, had not been drawing professionally since 1913. In her unpublished memoirs, Cory recalls an incident from her life at the time; an incident that sounds like something from a John Wayne movie:

Fred my husband, had gone for the mail (seven miles away) taking our daughter (Sayre) and the girl who had recently come to work for us with him for the ride—I knew her very nice mother quite well, and her drunken father by hearsay—our small son (Robert) was asleep in the bedroom.

A thundering knock at the door, door bursting open very drunk gentleman in the doorway—"Where is my girl, ha? Come on. where is she, no use hiding out ya know, I demand my daughter! Dede, where are ya? Lookye here, you're Fred Cooney's woman as thinks to make a hired girl of my daughter, are

The Kewpies, Rose O'Neill, 1935

"BEN BOLT"—The Kid That You Were Yourself

Don't you remember our dances, Ben Bolt,
And the feeling so hard to express,
When dear little Sue was so smitten with you,
That she hardly knew how to say "Yes."

Left: *"Ben Bolt"–The Kid That You Were Yourself,*
Fanny Y. Cory, 1916
Above: Fanny Y. Cory in later years
Below: *Other People's Children,* **Fanny Y. Cory, 1925**

Of course, the minister's wife had to send the children over on the very afternoon Evilan's mama had her poker club. It's hard these days to keep up with both the church and society.

ya? Do ya see these here scars on my face? Do ya see this 'ere gun? I know how t'use it, maam—now where's my daughter?"

To all of this I managed to turn a cold eye and indifferent aspect. "You had better go away from here as fast as you can or when my husband comes in he will no doubt beat the life out of you" (and more to this effect). He seemed to think there might be something in what I said and began to lurch out, still loudly asserting his demands for his daughter, he had a horse outside and managing to climb on, rode away—I began to shake all over and to cry, not so brave after all.

In 1916, Fanny Y. Cory briefly produced a single panel cartoon called *Ben Bolt,* parodying the old song "Do You Remember Sweet Alice, Ben Bolt?", but by 1925, the need to put her eldest child through college prompted her to return to her art permanently, this time in the form of first a single panel cartoon, and finally, a comic strip. Her first panel was the hilarious *Other People's Children,* although the almost too precious *Sonny Sayings,* from 1926, remained the artist's favorite. By 1935 Cory was producing another classic Depression strip, *Little Miss Muffet.* As mentioned earlier, cheerful little orphan girls were very big during the Depression. *Little Orphan Annie* and *Little Annie Rooney* (and

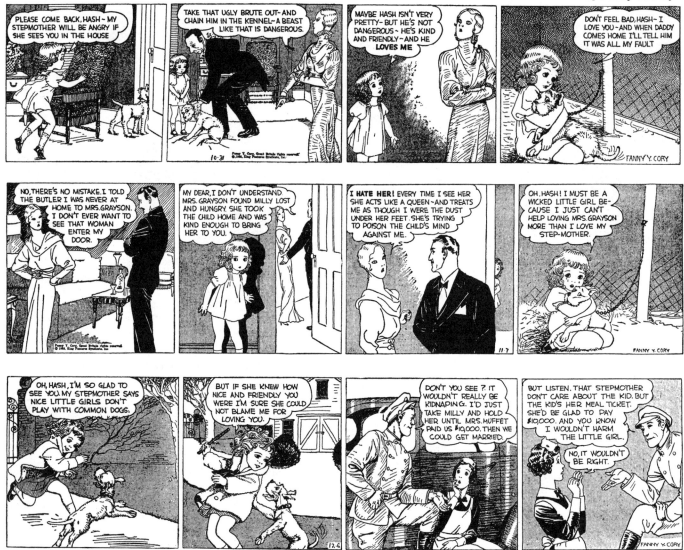

Little Miss Muffet, **Fanny Y. Cory, 1935**

their respective dogs) had a huge following. Cory's heroine, Milly Muffet, had a dog too, and was a dead ringer for Shirley Temple. The little darling smiled through her tears for twenty-one years, finally retiring when 76-year-old Cory's failing eyesight forced her to stop drawing in 1956. The artist moved to Camano Island, Washington, where despite her poor sight, she continued to paint. At the age of 90 she wrote:

I live alone in a two-room cottage on the edge of an 80-foot bank above Puget Sound. The broad sweep of water before me —then Mercer Island and behind that the peaks of the Olympic mountains snowtopped at most times. Mt. Olympus right directly across— then to my right if I face the Sound—the wood, lovely tall straight cedar pine and fir—thick underbrush—no attempt at cultivation. My road...is winding and full of potholes for the rain to collect...my place is a painful contrast to my neighbors— upon which not even a fallen leaf

Above: Fanny Y. Cory. A self-portrait of the artist with her characters

Top Right: Grace Drayton at the age of 50

Right: *Bobby as Napoleon,* Grace Drayton, 1932. In his biography *This Is Where I Came In,* Drayton collaborator Ed Anthony describes the artist's paintings: "Mrs. Drayton, proud of having originated the Campbell Kids, had done oil paintings of George Washington, Napoleon, Mark Twain and other great figures, in which their figures were recognizable even though they emerged as pink-cheeked Campbell cherubs."

is allowed to be. No underbrush there…How they must shudder at such a neighbor—and yet they are, I'm sure, fond of me and always willing to lend a hand should I need help…

Fanny Y. Cory died in 1972 at the age of 95.

Meanwhile Grace Drayton, the other contemporary of O'Neill and Cory, had fallen upon hard times. Like the carefree flappers, Drayton's *Dimples and Dingles,* with their nannies and nursies, seemed out of place in Depression America. Her Sunday comic page, *Dolly Dimples and Bobby Bounce,* had been canceled in 1932 and the following year when her assistant, Bernard Wagner, wrote asking for work, she sent him this reply:

"I have no work and am almost down and out. I have tried

·BOBBY·AS·NAPOLEON·

·THE·LITTLE·GREAT·MASTERS·

Above: *The Pussycat Princess,* Grace Drayton, 1935

Opposite page–

Top: *The Pussycat Princess,* Ed Anthony and Ruth Carroll, 1936

Bottom: *Sister Susie,* Alice Harvey, 1936. Harvey, better known as a cartoonist for *The New Yorker,* did this short-lived cute girl strip for the New York *Daily News*

Cindy of the Hotel Royale, Mazie Krebs, 1927. Krebs' Depression-era protagonist differs from her flapper sisters of the previous decade in that she works for a living.

Weegee, unsold strip by Dale Messick, circa 1927

everything. You may rest assured I shall send for you if I get another 'job.' I feel so sad whenever I look at our empty studio. To add to my agony, I lost my only dearly beloved sister a few weeks ago. So I am now all alone and poverty stricken in heart as well as in pocket."

But Drayton did rally one last time to successfully sell *The Pussycat Princess* in 1935. Her collaborator on the strip, writer Ed Anthony, gallantly writes that after Drayton's untimely death from a heart attack one year later, "...nearly all the big papers cancelled, which gave me a pretty good notion as to why it had been accepted in the first place." Ruth Carroll, a children's book writer and illustrator, took over the strip, but, writes Anthony, "we lacked the promotion value of the Drayton name...and we were unable to regain the big papers we had lost."

Anthony was being kind. The truth is that *The Pussycat Princess* drawn by Ruth Carroll did well, lasting until 1947, and

that at first the strips done with Drayton didn't even credit her; they simply read "by Ed Anthony." The great Grace Drayton, creator of the Campbell Kids and in her time the favorite of millions, had become passé.

An exception to the unfortunate tradition of ending one's career in favor of marriage and motherhood was *Brenda Starr* creator Dale Messick, probably one of the most seriously committed and tenacious woman cartoonists of the century. In a 1973 newspaper interview she describes her pregnancy: "It was throw up, draw *Brenda,* throw up, draw *Brenda.*" Before she sold the long-lasting strip that was to make her the *grande dame* of comics, Messick attempted to sell at least four others. Born Dalia Messick, the artist likes to relate that she changed her name to the more sexually ambiguous Dale because editors would reject her strips and then put the make on her. The way she finally sold *Brenda,* she says in all her

Mimi the Mermaid, unsold strip by Dale Messick, early 1930s

Peg and Pudy, the Strugglettes, unsold strip by Dale Messick, mid-1930s

interviews, was to become Dale and mail the strips in. However, only the first of her unsold strips, *Weegee,* drawn probably when the artist was just out of high school in the mid-1920s, is signed Dalia. The other three, all drawn during the '30s, are already credited to her new name, Dale. So there must be another reason why they were rejected. It's certainly not the art; even Messick's first strip is at least as well drawn as some of the flapper strips from the period. What makes *Weegee* different from those strips is the subject matter. As previously stated, the heroines of the flapper strips never had a care in the world; only Virginia Huget's characters even held a job, and they had a way of inheriting money from rich relatives. Weegee is a Depression strip heroine born ahead of her time, a poor little country girl come to the big city to earn a living.

By the time she was drawing and attempting to sell *Mimi the Mermaid,* Messick's drawing style had improved immensely, but editors must have found her subject matter simply too weird. Not until 1990, with Walt Disney's *The Little Mermaid,* has there ever been a comic starring a mermaid. This time, Messick was roughly sixty years ahead of her time.

With the creation of *Peg and Pudy, the Strugglettes,* it looked like Messick was catching up with the times—or vice versa. *Struglettes* metamorphosed into *Streamline Babies,* with the same characters and the same situations—two girls attempting to make it in the Big City. At last it looked like the persistent artist had finally hit it; the McNaught syndicate showed an interest in her strip. But after Messick had completed three Sunday pages, the syndicate decided to go instead with an Edgar Bergen and Charlie McCarthy strip. Comic editors appear to have always been

Streamline Babies, unsold strips by Dale Messick, circa 1938.

a conservative lot, and still today will always buy a strip starring a licensed character rather than take a chance on an unknown. Messick remembers trying to be brave when she was told the news, but finally, unable to control herself, with tears running down her cheeks, she told the editor that a comic about a wooden dummy would never last.

She was right—the strip folded within a month. But by that time, Dale Messick was busily at work creating the right strip for the right time.

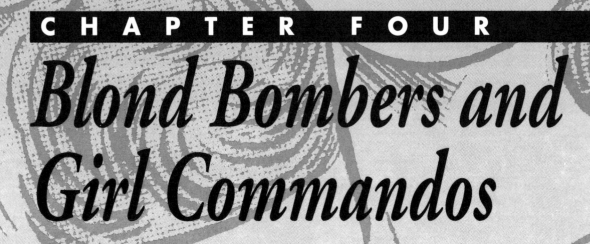

MUST BE A CONCEALED PANEL
AP DOOR THAT LET THEM
ANOTHER PART OF THE SHIP.

CHAPTER FOUR

Blond Bombers and Girl Commandos

Above: *The Monastery of the Blue God,* Cecilia Paddock Munson, *Adventure Comics,* June, 1937

Right: *Daredevil Barry Finn,* Tarpe Mills, *Amazing Mystery Funnies,* September, 1939

America in 1940 not to enter World War II for another year, the majority of citizens sympathized with the Allies, and since the mid-'30s, Americans had volunteered to fight Fascism overseas. Movies, pulp fiction, and the new medium of comic books all echoed the action-oriented theme of war and preparing for war. Almost from the beginning, comic books were employing women.

In the June, 1937, issue of *Adventure Comics,* Cecilia Paddock Munson, signing her work "Pad," illustrated *The Monastery of the Blue God,* a spy story involving stolen Swedish military secrets, Bolsheviki, and the beauteous Baroness Elsa Von Saxenberg. Two years later, Tarpe Mills, who in 1942 was to produce one of the best action strips of the century, was drawing *Daredevil Barry Finn* for *Amazing Mystery Funnies.* The comic's villain, Doctor Zaroff, tried to sell Hitler and Mussolini an infernal invention that "can prevent the United States from interfering with your plans for war!!" The fiendish plot is foiled by Finn with help from his friend Joan Hart, a young woman who looks exactly like Mills' later costumed heroine, *Miss Fury.*

America was ready for a strong, action-oriented heroine, and Dale Messick was at last in the right place at the right time with *Brenda Starr,* her red-haired, starry-eyed girl reporter. Messick's sample strips had been submitted to Captain Joseph M. Patterson, publisher of the New York *Daily News* and chief of the Chicago Tribune-New York News Syndicate, and rejected by him. The reason given, according to a 1960 article in *The Saturday Evening Post,* was that "He had tried a woman cartoonist once...and wanted no

One of New Saturday Green Flash Features

BRENDA STARR
☆☆☆☆
PLUCKY REDHEADED
GIRL REPORTER
FOR THE **FLASH**

TOM TAYLOR
☆☆☆
CRACK CAMERAMAN,
IN LOVE
WITH BRENDA

PESKY MILLER
☆
COPY BOY

DAPHNE DIMPLES
☆☆☆
THE BOSS'S NIECE,
RICH, PAMPERED, AND A
BORN TROUBLE MAKER

MUGGS WALTERS
☆☆☆☆
THE BOSS AND EDITOR
OF THE **FLASH**.
UNDER HIS GRUFF
MANNER THERE IS
A HEART OF GOLD

Dale Messick

We'd like to have you meet a new "reporter" on The Call-Bulletin—Brenda Starr. Technically speaking, of course, she's a reporter for the "Flash," and she's the heroine of a thrilling new comic strip in full color which will be a regular feature of the Saturday Green Flash.

Brenda has a lot of playmates in this new comic page, and they're formally introduced above. In addition to the regular comic, each Saturday installment of "Brenda Starr" will include fashion cut-outs in full color for the kiddies.

And Brenda is just one of many new features which will appear regularly in the Saturday Green Flash. "Black Fury," a thrilling new adventure comic, has been added. Both Orphan Annie and Winnie Winkle will be published in a big new Saturday size. Also the popular Chesnutt-Parks feature, "First Families at the Films," returns to the Saturday Green Flash as a regular feature.

These are all new features in addition to the many regular Call-Bulletin features and comics.

Get your big weekend paper with all the new features tomorrow!

Top: Panel from the San Francisco *Call-Bulletin,* October 31, 1941, announcing the addition of *Brenda Starr* to its comics page.

Above: The first episode of *Brenda Starr, Reporter,* by Dale Messick, 1940

Top: Brenda and her Mystery Man. A particularly lush, romantic panel from 1960.

Above: Dale Messick in 1955

Opposite page: *Brenda Starr,* 1963, Dale Messick. This page was drawn for the *New York Daily News,* to inform readers about what they had missed during a long newspaper strike.

more of them." Mollie Slott, at the time Patterson's "Girl Friday" and later vice president and manager of the syndicate, found the discarded samples and recognized the potential in them. Together, she and Messick worked out a new submission. The heroine, named after glamorous debutante Brenda Frazier, had originally been a "girl bandit." Heeding Slott's advice, the artist turned her into a reporter.

Patterson grudgingly agreed to carry *Brenda Starr* in his syndicate, but flatly refused to run it in the *Daily News.* Indeed, The *News* did not carry *Brenda Starr* until two years after Patterson's death in 1946.

Patterson was not the only male to have it in for Messick's creation. Although the strip inspired a huge female following from the beginning (when the Tucson *Daily Citizen* dropped the strip in 1973, the editors received hundreds of angry letters and phone calls, the majority of which were from women), the artist never felt fully accepted by her male colleagues, and she resisted joining the National Cartoonists Society. As *The Saturday Evening Post* article delicately put it when writing about the male cartoonists' attitudes, "There are differences of opinion about her artistic talents." In a 1973 newspaper interview, Messick wryly gave her opinion of the mostly male organization: "I see where they're honoring Jack Dempsey. They never honored me for anything, but they honor Jack Dempsey."

Even the writer of the 1960 *Post* article felt compelled to belittle Messick by stressing her "wacky dame" aspects. Here is a description of a typical day in the artist's studio: "The hi-fi is on full blast. Miss Messick sings along lustily. If the music is appropriate, she jumps up and does a rhumba. In meditative periods she chews gum with popping sound effects."

Messick's heroine, whose looks were based on film star Rita Hayworth's, parachuted from planes, joined girl gangs, escaped from kidnappers, almost froze to

Above: Brenda joins a teen gang in 1956.

enced by Nell Brinkley's, is romantic and feminine. Yet she drew action scenes excellently, and offered the reader a memorable cast of supporting characters: Flip Decker, teenage leader of an all-blonde girl gang; The Nameless Doll, a pouf-haired Robin Hood; Palava, the albino Polynesian princess, and of course the handsome, one-eyed Mystery Man. Chester Gould's *Dick Tracy*, again carried by the same syndicate, boasted of equally, if not more bizarre, supporting characters. But of his art, James Steranko had this to say in his 1970 book, *The Steranko History of Comics*: "His drawings had about as much depth as a cardboard cut-out. As a technician, he would be out-distanced by miles. If Gould had any knowledge of perspective he kept it to himself."

Why then this negativity aimed against Messick's creation on the part of men in the industry? As demonstrated, there had been plenty of women drawing comics for the past forty years, and there is no record of men strongly criticizing their work. However, all the previous comics by women had been comparatively light—cute animals and kids, pretty girls without a care in the world, rotund grandmas spouting homespun death on snow-covered slopes, and got marooned on desert islands.

Meanwhile, *The Gumps*, a strip created by Patterson, which moved as slowly as molasses and must be called boring by the kindest critic, had been carried by the same syndicate since 1919.

Messick's drawing style, strongly influ-

Miss Fury, Tarpe Mills, 1943. Featuring General Bruno, and introducing Era.

Below: Dale Messick, Brenda in a parachute, circa 1950s.

philosophy. These comics might be considered "girl stuff"—a genre the men didn't care to work in or took seriously. But with *Brenda Starr*, Dale Messick was trespassing on male territory.

Messick opened the way for over a decade of action heroines in the comics. A year later, *Wonder Woman*, the creation of psychologist William Moulton Marston and artist Harry G. Peter, hit the newsstands in the December, 1941, issue of *All Star Comics*. The immortal amazon was the first costumed action heroine in comic books, but it would be 45 years before she was drawn by a woman.

Beating *Wonder Woman* for the title of first costumed action heroine in any form of comics was Tarpe Mills' *Miss Fury*, which made its debut as a newspaper strip in April, 1941, eight months before the birth of Moulton's creation. Since 1938, Mills had been contributing to comic books with such characters as *The Purple Zombie*, *Devil's Dust*, and *The*

Tarpe Mills and her cat, Perri-Purr.

Cat Man. Born June Mills, like Dale Messick, she changed her name to a sexually ambiguous one, taking the name Tarpe upon entering the comics field. In a newspaper interview from the 1940s, she said, "It would have been a major letdown to the kids if they found out that the author of such virile and awesome characters was a gal."

Mills' gender did not stay secret for long. As her strip gained in popularity, newspapers carried articles about it, always including photos of its creator, who bore a startling resemblance to her protagonist, Marla Drake, the socialite who becomes Miss Fury upon donning a form-fitting panther skin.

Just as Messick had identified with her creation to the point of dyeing her own hair red and naming her daughter Starr, Mills put not only herself, but also her cat, into the strip. Both the artist and her protagonist had white Persian cats named Perri-Purr.

In 1945, the Miami *Daily News* ran a story titled, "Cartoon Strip Cat Goes Off To War," relating that Tarpe Mills had donated her cat to the war effort. Subtitled, "It's Sir Admiral Purr Now," the article related how Mills' Persian had become the mascot of an allied warship, and "...set out for distant places and unknown dangers, sound asleep in the commander's bunk." The article goes on to make it clear that the famous cat had the attitude of all cats through history: "'I'd be happier if he'd show a little emotion,' [Mills] said, before parting with the newly made admiral."

Tarpe Mills' years at New York's Pratt Institute, during which she modeled to pay her way through school, along with her early years in comics, stood her in good stead. From its first episode, *Miss Fury* was beautifully drawn. Like Messick, Mills filled her panels with glamour; both artists liked to depict their woman characters in frilly lingerie or in bubble baths. Mills' strip was at times considered *too* racy. One episode, in which a character wore the equivalent of a bikini, so shocked the editors of 37 newspapers that they canceled the strip that day. At a time when the average male cartoonist dressed his heroines in plain red dresses, the women cartoonists were paying attention to clothes. The continuities of *Miss Fury*, and those of *Brenda Starr*, can double as textbooks on fashions of the 1940s. Mills' strips, reminiscent of *film noir*, take the reader from the chic penthouses and nightclubs of wartime New York to underground Nazi installations and anti-Nazi guerrilla camps in Brazil. Along the way the reader meets some of the most unforgettable characters in the history of comics: Erica Von Kampf, the platinum blond adventuress with a swastika branded on her forehead; Albino Jo, the Harvard-educated albino Indian;

December 5th, 1942.

Dear Don:

Much as I'd like to, I cannot send you an original page . . . You see, Don, after the pages are used in the newspapers, they are later on reprinted in comic books, the first of which (entitled Miss Fury) should be on the newsstands within the next week. However, because of the number of requests for special drawings, pin-up girls, cutout dolls, fashions, etc., I believe the publisher of the magazine has also printed additional drawings which can be mailed to those requesting them.

Now, about the schools: Yep! I took an art course at Erasmus Hall High School and later went to Pratt Institute on Ryerson Street . . . and I see no reason why, if you're really set on it, you couldn't supplement your high school studies with a night course at some good art school.

Incidentally, the drawings in the school book you sent me last summer looked quite good. Have you ever tried brushes instead of pens? . . . I think you'll find the work goes faster, dries quicker and has a freer line.

Best wishes,

Yours sincerely,
Tarpé Mills
Tarpé Mills

Above: A letter from Tarpe Mills to a fan, 12-year-old Donald Goldsamt. The *Miss Fury* comic books of which she writes, sold over a million copies per issue, and would have had even wider circulation if production of books had not been limited by the wartime paper shortage. Today a successful Marvel comic book sells about 400,000 copies. Other Sunday newspaper strips that were re-pasted into comic books were *Brenda Starr, Little Miss Muffet, Mopsy,* and *Teena* by Hilda Terry.

Left: This panel, from a 1947 *Miss Fury* comic strip, was considered too racy for 37 newspapers, which cancelled the strip that day.

Brazilian bombshell Era, and the one armed German General Bruno Beitz.

Because of this last character, *Miss Fury* got attention in the January 4, 1943 issue of *Time* magazine. An article, "Comic-strip Generals," likened "One-armed, egg-bald 'General Bruno' [who] is frustrated by Brazilian guerrillas in his campaign to open the way for an Axis invasion" to "his counterpart... mysterious General Gunther Niedenfuhr,...military attache in Brazil."

Miss Fury lasted through 1952, but Tarpe Mills was not finished with comics. In 1971, she returned briefly to illustrate a seven page romance strip in Marvel Comics' *Our Love Story.* Unfortunately, her attempt to update her *noir* styling into something mod resulted in the equivalent of a vintage Joan Crawford dress that has been cut down into a mini. From 1979 until her death in 1988, the artist attempted unsuccessfully to sell a comic based on her wartime hero, Albino Jo. Sample pages demonstrate that Mills never lost her artistic touch, but editors in the 1980s were not receptive to the nostalgic look of her art.

There is a widely held belief that women cartoonists worked under male

Miss Fury (left), 1943, and *Model With a Broken Heart* (below), by Tarpe Mills, from *Our Love Story*, December, 1971. Compare this page with the page from 1943.

pseudonyms in order to sell their comic strips. This is only partially true. As seen, Rose O'Neill, Grace Drayton, Ethel Hays, Nell Brinkley and their contemporaries had no trouble getting published under their own feminine names. However, a male pseudonym did seem to be required for action strips, starting with Caroline Sexton who, in 1934, signed "C.M. Sexton" to *Luke and Duke.* From Cecilia Paddock Munson, who often signed her work either "Pad" or "Paddock Munson," to Ramona "Pat" Patenaude, to Dale Messick and Tarpe Mills, the women of the '40s seemed to believe their success depended at least in part upon a male name.

Another woman who took a masculine name was Mabel Burwick; at the start of her career, she changed her name to Odin Burvik. Originally hired as assistant to cartoonist Coulton Waugh, by 1944 she had not only taken over his strip, *Dickie Dare,* but also married him. In the tradition of Marjorie Henderson ("Marge") and Edwina Dumm ("Edwina"), the artist signed her strip with her first name, "Odin."

Messick and Mills had changed their names to disguise their gender. Neysa McMein, born Marjorie, changed hers because she was advised to do so by a numerologist. A popular illustrator and portrait artist, McMein painted every cover of *McCall's* magazine from 1923 through 1938, and designed Gold Medal flour's

Page from an unpublished comic by Tarpe Mills, 1979.

Top: Cover from *Mc Call's* magazine, 1936, Neysa McMein.

Above: *Dickie Dare*, Odin Burvik, circa 1944-45. Like the *Miss Fury* Sunday pages, this has been re-pasted and reprinted in comic book form in *Famous Funnies*.

trademark character, Betty Crocker, in 1936.

McMein had always been avant garde in her lifestyle. In the teens, she had marched in pro-suffrage demonstrations, and in the '20s, she was a member of the illustrious Algonquin Round Table. This group of well-known writers and artists, who met at New York's Algonquin Hotel, included such luminaries as Dorothy Parker, Harpo Marx and Alexander Woollcott.

The latter described her in an article for *McCall's*, 1933. He mentions a play called *The Joy of Living*, and continues: "I never knew what the phrase meant until I met Neysa McMein. And of the girls she draws for you, one and all, dark and fair, grave or gay, you know this one thing—that, like herself, they are enormously pleased with the privilege of being alive."

If that sounds like the author may have been a little in love with his subject, the supposition is correct. In 1923, learning that McMein was on a ship about to depart for Europe, Woollcott boarded it, intending to propose to her. It was then that he learned that she had just married John Baragwanath, a mining engineer, and that the two of them were headed for separate honeymoons—she to Europe, and he to an expedition in Quebec. (Thanks to McMein's many journalist friends, her unusual honeymoon prompted a flurry of newspaper and magazine articles with headlines like "A New Groom Sleeps Clean.")

Eventually this successful and unconventional woman tried her hand at a comic strip. *Deathless Deer*, drawn by McMein and written by newspaper pub-

Neysa McMein, from a photo in *McCall's* magazine, 1933.

Advertisement for *Deathless Deer, Seattle Post-Intelligencer*, 1942.

lisher Alicia Patterson, made its newspaper debut in November, 1942. (Patterson, the daughter of Joseph Patterson, had also figured in the Dale Messick saga when, her father refusing to run *Brenda Starr*, she had carried it in her newspaper, the Long Island *Free Press*. After Joseph Patterson died, and the editors of the *Daily News* wanted to carry the strip, they tried to convince Alicia Patterson to drop it, because major newspapers prefer not to share their strips with smaller newspapers in surrounding neighborhoods. But Patterson refused to part with *Brenda Starr*, and the strip appeared in both papers at the same time, an almost unheard-of occurrence.)

An advertisement for *Deathless Deer* in the Seattle *Post-Intelligencer*, on November 1, 1942, describes it perfectly:

Princess Deer, beautiful, imperi-

ous, dangerous, occupied the throne of the Egyptian kings 3,000 years ago.

Her word was law, her wealth boundless, her beauty drove men mad.

But she had enemies.

One tried to slay her for her treasure—but was foiled by the high priest who gave Princess Deer a potion which caused her to sleep three thousand years.

Then she awakes in the present-day world—and meets Bruce, a handsome young engineer... and thus is off to adventure, romance, love.

Today, *Deathless Deer* has fallen into

**Deathless Deer,
Neysa McMein, 1942**

total obscurity. One male collector has suggested that the strip was forgotten because the concept was so implausible. However, the story of a mummy coming back to life thousands of year later, done successfully in the mummy movies of the '30s, and more recently by novelist Anne Rice, is no more ridiculous than the idea of a baby from outer space landing on Earth and growing up to be Superman.

By 1942, America had gone to war. Most of the men drawing for comic books at that time were of draft age, and like men in all other industries in the country, they either volunteered or were drafted into the military. And, as in every other industry, women took their places. That year, the number of women working for comic books tripled, and the numbers stayed high until the end of the '40s.

Few women drew the costumed heroes that had become so popular since the birth of *Superman* in 1938. Some exceptions were Ramona ("Pat") Patenaude, who drew *Blue Beetle, V-Man, The Green Falcon, Dr. Fung,* and *The Vision* during the early '40s, and Peggy Zangerle, who drew *Doc Savage* and *Red Dragon* in 1948.

And in 1947, Nina Albright drew *The Cadet*, starring Kit Carter, for *Target Comics*. Although *The Cadet* had a male lead, it included strong female characters, in response to letters sent in by mostly female readers asking for "special girl characters." The comic book printed a letter from Virginia Warsachi, of Omaha, Nebraska, who wrote: "Don't you think it would be a good idea to have a heroine in *Target* for a change?"; and Sally Foos, of Warren, Ohio, wrote : "I think it would be very nice if there were some girls as it would make the comic more exciting."

Most women artists seem to excel at drawing female characters, and that is what most of them did. Typical wartime heroine titles were *Yankee Girl*, drawn by Ann Brewster, or *Blond Bomber* and *Girl Commandos*, drawn by both Barbara Hall in 1942, and by Jill Elgin from 1942-45. And in 1946 and 1947, Janice Valleau drew *Toni Gayle*, a glamorous fashion model/detective character, for *Young King Cole* comics.

Gladys Parker's *Mopsy* got into the act, and for the duration could be seen in her comics in the uniform of a Waac, a Wave, an army nurse, and a member of the Motor Corps. Parker also took over the newspaper strip *Flyin' Jenny* when its regular artist, Russell Keaton, went into the service in 1943. Jenny was a blond aviatrix

The Cadet, Nina Albright, from **Target Comics,** October, 1947.

who, like many wartime heroines, battled Nazis.

Of all the comic book companies in the '40s, one publisher hired more women cartoonists than any of the others. That was Fiction House, a company started in 1936 by Jerry Iger and Will Eisner, artist/creator of *The Spirit* comic strip.

Girl Commandos, Jill Elgin, published by Harvey Comics, early 1940s.

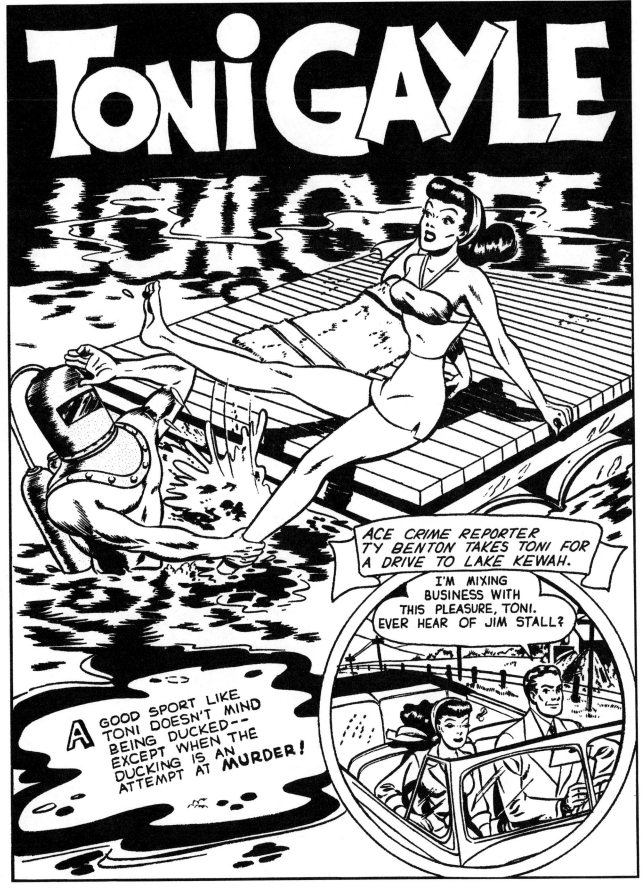

Toni Gayle, Janice Valeau, from *Young King Cole Comics,* 1947.

Mopsy joins the armed services. Gladys Parker, 1944-45.

The six Fiction House comic book titles— *Jumbo, Jungle, Fight, Wings, Rangers* and *Planet*—specialized in luridly sensationalistic stories with strong and beautiful female protagonists. Unlike comics from some of the other publishers, where the female characters seemed to exist only as foils for the hero to rescue, these women were in charge. Depending on the comic, they could be jungle girls, pilots, "girl detectives," or outer space heroines. Dressed in two-piece leopard skin bathing suits or ripped Army nurse uniforms, they leaped across the page in a graphic role-reversal, guns blazing or knife in hand, to rescue some man. And they were likely to be drawn by women. Jean Levander and

Fran Hopper drew the "girl detective" strip *Glory Forbes*; Ann Brewster and Fran Hopper drew *Jane Martin*, who started out as a war nurse and wound up as an aviatrix; Marcia Snyder and, once more, Fran Hopper, drew the jungle heroine *Camilla*. For Fiction Houses's science fiction title,

Above: *Flyin' Jenny*, 1944. Although credited to Russell Keaton, the art is by Gladys Parker.
Below: Sketch of Fran Hopper by Lily Renee, circa mid-1940s.

Planet Comics, the prolific Hopper drew *Gale Allen and Her All Girl Squadron* and *Mysta of the Moon*. While Mysta was a sort of goddess who lived on our satellite, the All Girl squadron were more like Waacs of the future, battling evil on other planets. Like many female artists, Hopper drew women beautifully, but her weak point was men. These stories, with mostly female characters, suited her perfectly.

Unquestionably the star woman cartoonist on the Fiction House staff, and the only woman who ever drew a cover for them, was Lily Renee. From 1943 through 1948, her elegant art graced the pages of their books. Although she contributed some light and "cartoony" filler pages, such as *Tess Taxi*, her best work could be seen in *The Lost World*, *Senorita Rio*, and *Werewolf Hunters*. *The Lost World*, the lead story in *Planet Comics*, took place in a post-apocalyptic future. Amid ruins of New York City a plucky group of survivors, led by Hunt Bowman and his fetchingly ragged companion, Lyssa, battled the Voltamen, their green-skinned and Nazi-like alien conquerors. *Senorita Rio*, who starred in *Fight Comics*, was a Brazilian nightclub

GLORY FORBES IN EVERY ISSUE OF RANGERS COMICS!!

Glory Forbes, Fran Hopper, *Rangers Comics*, October, 1945

Camilla,
Marcia Snyder,
Jungle Comics,
circa mid-1940s.

The Lost World,
Lily Renee,
Planet Comics,
circa mid-1940s

entertainer who fought Nazis in her spare time. The character bore a strong resemblance to Tarpe Mills' Brazilian anti-Nazi guerrilla leader, Era. Lily Renee was another artist whose renderings of women far surpassed that of men, and *Werewolf Hunters*, a horror/fantasy strip, inspired some of her most decorative and imaginative art, with stories that often involved some mystic or supernatural woman character.

While newspaper strips had usually been written and drawn by the same person, the comic book industry was less personal, and none of the women cartoonists wrote the strips they drew. In the case of Fiction House, the stories were often written by a woman, too. From 1940, when she was only twenty years old, until 1961, Ruth Roche, sometimes using the male pseudonym "Rod Roche," was first the company's major writer, and later editor. Although women writers worked for both Fiction House and other comic book companies, Roche probably wrote more comics during the '40s than any other woman who was not also drawing her own strip.

When the war ended, women in every industry were encouraged to vacate their jobs in favor of the returning men. In the world of comics, where women had been working since 1901, the back-to-the-kitchen movement took a different form. Although women continued to draw lighter strips through the '50s, the men took back their action comics. By 1952, when *Miss Fury* ended, *Brenda Starr* was the only adventure strip that starred a woman and was drawn by a woman. The women had stopped drawing action strips.

Above: *Skull Squad*, from *Wings Comics*, published by Fiction House, early 1940s. Art by Ruth Atkinson. Not all of Fiction House's women artists got to draw heroines, but on this page artist Atkinson manages to get drawings of pretty women into an otherwise all-male story.

Top left: Self-portrait of Lily Renee, mid-1940s.

Above: Lily Renee. Previously unpublished panels from *Senorita Rio, Fight Comics,* mid-1940s. One panel had been inked, the other partially pencilled, when Renee was asked by the editor to substitute another panel. These panels were pasted over, and have never before been printed.

Left: *Mopsy,* Gladys Parker, 1945. *Mopsy,* like thousands of other women, prepares to leave her war job.

Opposite and following pages –

Lily Renee, from *Rangers Comics,* 1948. Some very strong women characters emerged from comics of the forties. In this one, sisterhood (or aunthood) is powerful, and the unexpected strong character is an old woman.

The WEREWOLF HUNTER
by ARMAND BROUSSARD

THE CHAIR CREAKED AND CANDLES FLICKERED AS AUNT HETTY SAT BY HER MISER'S COFFIN AND STITCHED ON THE BRIDAL DRESS OF HER LONG-LOST LOVE... SHE WAS A QUEER ONE, OLD HETTY WAS, AND PERHAPS THAT IS WHY SHE COULD LAUGH TO HEAR THE TAP-TAP-TAP OF DEATH AT THE DOOR —

L. Renée

SOFT WORDS AND SLY SMILES FOR THEIR DAFT OLD AUNT— BUT I KNOW WHAT'S IN THEIR HEARTS, BIXBY! I KNOW THEIR TRICKS! I'LL RING WHEN I'M READY FOR 'EM...

YOUR NIECE AND NEPHEWS TO SEE YOU, MA'AM.

HEH-HEH-HEH! COME TO BEG MORE MONEY, EH?

CHAPTER FIVE
Tradition

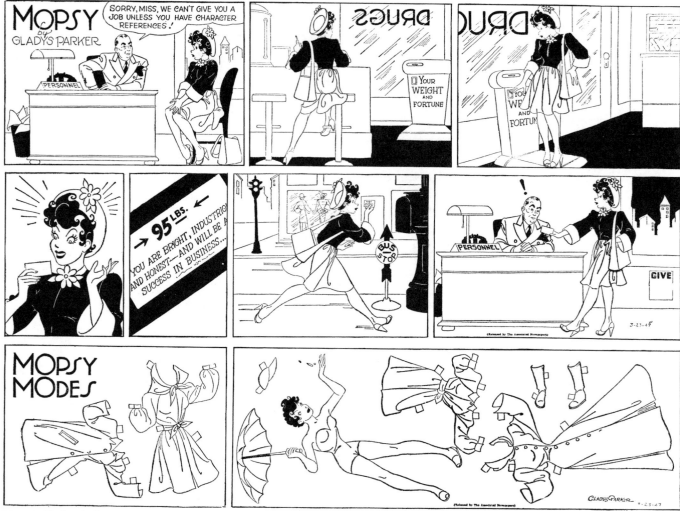

Mopsy, **Gladys Parker, 1947. Mopsy, fired from her defense job after the War like thousands of other women, looks for new employment.**

Gladys Parker, circa 1950.

All during the 1940s, of course, women were still drawing comics about children, as they had been doing since the beginning of the century. Now, with the advent of action-oriented comic books, came action strips featuring children. As early as 1938, Claire S. Moe drew a series of children's adventure strips with circus-related themes for Centaur's *Funny Pages. The Circus and Sue, Circus Days,* and *Little Mary of the Circus* were all exciting serials reminiscent of films from the period featuring Shirley Temple.

That same year, Corrinne Boyd Dillon produced a strip called *Jigger,* and Jean Hotchkiss drew one called *Donnie Stuart,* both for Globe's *Circus, the Comic Riot.* Despite the book's title, these comics were not about the circus; both strips told the story of a young boy, one with his dog,

The Circus and Sue, Claire S. Moe, 1938

Above: *Land of the Lost,* drawn by Olive Bailey, written by Isabel Manning Hewson, 1947.

Top right: Olive Bailey, 1947

and one with his sister.

In 1946 and '47, the team of writer Isabel Manning Hewson and artist Olive Bailey adapted the popular radio program, *Land of the Lost,* into comic book form. The strip chronicled the adventures of two children, Isabel and Billy, in an undersea fantasy kingdom, pitting them against such villains as Spondo, leader of the notorious devilfish, and Uriah Slug.

And throughout the '40s, Vee Quintal Pearson illustrated a series of strips for Catholic comic books such as *Heroes All* and *Treasure Chest.* These comics, distributed free at parochial schools and churches, featured stories of saints and other role models for Catholic children.

Meanwhile, on the Sunday pages of the newspapers, it seemed as though all the cute kids from the early years of the century had finally grown into teenagers. The new teens of the '40s differed from the carefree coeds of the '20s and the sincere, hard-working depression kids. Clad in rolled-up dungarees and big shirts, they lounged around in rag doll positions, talking interminably on the phone. The girls moped about boys, and the boys, perpetually skinny, raided the refrigerators of their girlfriend's parents.

December 7, 1941 was not a day in which people were likely to spare much time for the funny pages of their local newspaper, so many Americans missed the debut of Hilda Terry's *Teena,* the first of many teen girl strips to be drawn by women throughout the next twenty-odd years. Terry's adorable bobby soxer survived the war and, in fact, lasted until 1966.

Teena had been running successfully for ten years when, in 1951, Hilda Terry's husband, cartoonist Gregory D'Alessio, proposed her name for membership in the National Cartoonists Society. Despite fifty years of women cartoonists, the NCS was still an all-male organization. Terry was blackballed, the reason given being

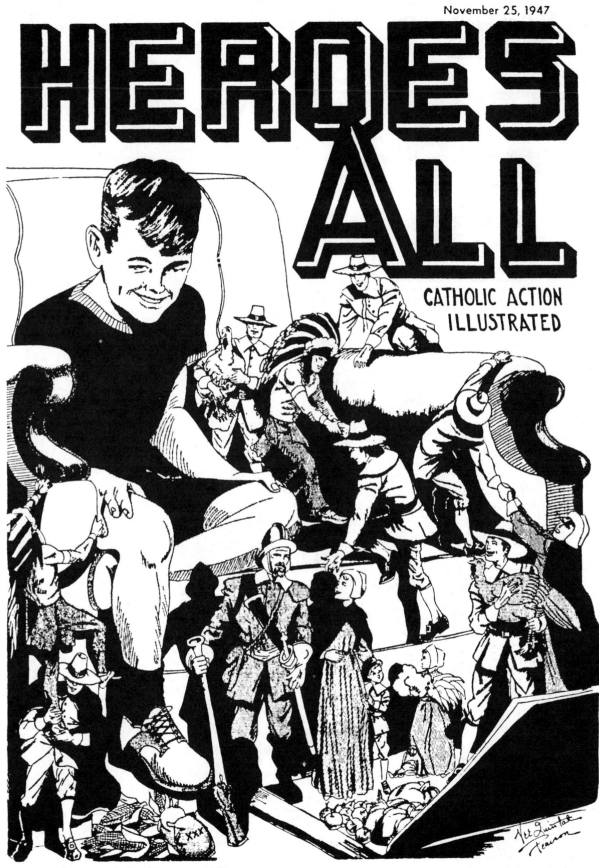

November 25, 1947

HEROES ALL

CATHOLIC ACTION ILLUSTRATED

Treasure Chest, Vee Quintal Pearson, 1947

Teena, Hilda Terry, 1954

Left: After World War II, Hilda Terry toured with an all-male group of cartoonists, entertaining the troops. The only problem with being the lone woman was that when she went to the ladies' room, the rest of the cartoonists would go on stage. One day she emerged from the lavatory to discover that the group had left the country without her.

Below: Hilda Terry, on the USO tour, dressed as Teena.

that if women were present at meetings of the prestigious group, the men wouldn't be able to curse. (Sadly, this was not the last time this excuse was used to exclude women from all-male groups. In a July 12, 1992 column for *The San Francisco Examiner*, journalist Stephanie Salter reminisced about how, in the late '60s, she was denied press box credentials to cover a football game for her college paper. She was told it was "for [her] own protection. The language in the press box gets pretty salty for a lady's sensibilities.")

Hilda Terry's blackballing by the National Cartoonists Society was not unanimous; several cartoonists objected to it vigorously and vociferously—among them Milton Caniff and Al Capp. The result was another vote, and this time, she was accepted into the organization. As soon as Terry became a member, she put forth the names of Gladys Parker and her other women cartoonist friends, thus breaking the gender barrier of the NCS. After the demise of her strip, Hilda Terry

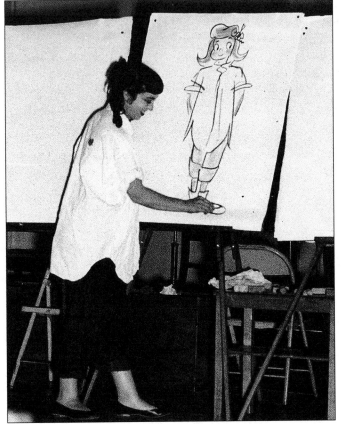

Above: *Bobby Sox,* and accompanying bottom strip, *Betty'n'Ho-Hum,* 1946, by Marty Links. Jerry Bendsen, Links' gag writer, also wrote for Hank Ketcham (*Dennis the Menace*), and columnist Herb Caen.

Right: Marty Links at the time she retired *Bobby Sox,* with her Cartoonist of the Year award.

went on to pioneer in yet another field, computer animation. Going from city to city, she animated caricatures of Major League baseball stars for sports stadium scoreboards around the country. Terry, who had wanted to be a sports cartoonist before doing *Teena,* finally attained her goal. And in 1979, she was given an award for best animation cartoonist from the same organization that had blackballed her almost thirty years before, the National Cartoonists Society. Today, although she could hardly be considered retired (she teaches classes twice a week at New York's Art Students League, and swims at the Y every day), she stays home

and writes.

The bobby soxer, a creation of the '40s, had by 1944 also become the name of a new teen strip by Marty Links, *Bobby Sox*. Links joined the National Cartoonists Society shortly after Hilda Terry, and found that even after she had sent the NCS an announcement of the birth of her first child, all the correspondence she received from them was still addressed to "Mr. Links." She admits to being annoyed enough to briefly consider mailing them her bust measurements.

While Hilda Terry, who had no children, got her inspiration from volunteer work with various girl groups—Blue Birds, Campfire Girls and American Youth Hostels—Marty Links had to look no further than her own home. When she needed to draw the classically messy bedroom of her character, Emmy Lou, she would just peer into the bedroom of her own teenaged daughter. Links decided to retire *Bobby Sox* in 1979, saying that she felt the strip no longer represented the teens of the day. Today she draws greeting cards for Hallmark, but at a time when there are so few newspaper strips by

women, and when even fewer are as well drawn as *Bobby Sox*, her strip is sorely missed.

A third comic, similar in style and equal in quality to *Teena* and *Bobby Sox*, was *Susie Q Smith*, drawn by Linda Walter and written by her husband, Jerry Walter. *Susie Q Smith* was syndicated to newspapers by King Features, and also had its own comic book, published by Dell.

The same year *Bobby Sox* started in newspapers, Virginia Clark, who had drawn so many beautiful flapper strips during the '20s and '30s under the name Virginia Huget, took over the strip *Oh,*

Left: Fashion illustrations by Hilda Terry, mid-1930s.

Above: *Susie Q. Smith*, art by Linda Walter, script by Jerry Walter, 1951.

Above: *Oh, Diana*, Virginia Clark, 1944.

Left: *Oh, Diana*, Virginia Clark. A promotional article from AP Features, the syndicate that distributed the strip.

Diana from cartoonist Don Flowers. Flowers, best known for his strip *Modest Maidens*, drew women in a uniquely pinup style. A promotional article from AP Features, the syndicate that distributed *Oh, Diana*, describes it as an adventure strip while drawn by Flowers. However, when Virginia Clark took it over, she turned it into another teen strip, "...to fit the trend," said the article, "toward pleasing youth." The amazingly versatile Clark, who ten years earlier had been able to perfectly mimic Percy Crosby's style, now changed her drawing to imitate Don Flowers.

It should be no surprise that a trait held in common by all these artists of teen strips was an acute awareness of fashion. Linda Walter, Hilda Terry and Marty Links had all worked in the fashion field before going on to comics, and another promotional article about Virginia Clark's *Oh, Diana* reads, "Diana's authentic, smartly-styled clothes have added appeal

Left: Ruth Atkinson,
Millie the Model #1,
1945.

Right: Ruth Atkinson, *Patsy Walker #2*, 1945. In this unusual story, done 25 years before the Woman's Liberation movement, Patsy realizes that boys get paid more than girls, and organizes a protest; she and her girlfriends break the high school's dress code by wearing slacks to class. On page 3, Patsy announces, "We're going to liberate all womankind!"

FASHION + POSE by BARBARA RAUSCH — TROPHY BY BILL WOGGON — CONGRATULATIONS, BARBARA!

Katy Keene pinup page by Cassie Bill, mid-1950s. Young Barbara Rausch, honored in this picture as "designer of the year," has become a successful comics artist herself today.

Above: Hazel Marten, drawing as "Scott Fleming." From *Nevada Jones,* written by Bill Woggon, *Pep Comics,* 1948.

Opposite page–
Top: *Taffy,* Phyllis Muchow, 1946.
Bottom: *Rusty,* by "Dottie," 1947.

for women readers."

It didn't take comic books long to catch up with newspaper strips. In 1945, Sergeant Stan Lee, newly mustered out of the armed forces, resumed his prewar position as editor and art director at a line of comic books published by his uncle, Martin Goodman. These books, bearing many different names, would eventually become Marvel comics, the largest comic book publisher in America. They included super hero titles and comics with a teen theme, aimed primarily at young girls. That same year, Ruth Atkinson, one of the many women who drew for Fiction House, had been promoted to art director. Unhappy with her new position, which left her unable to draw, she quit Fiction House and became a freelancer. Two of her first jobs were for the comic books edited by Lee, and consisted of drawing the first issues of both *Millie the Model* and *Patsy Walker*. Of all the teen comics edited by Lee for the next twenty, those two titles became the most successful and longest lasting. Although Atkinson only drew the first issue of *Millie the Model*, she stayed with *Patsy Walker* for the comic's first two years.

Martin Goodman also published a magazine called *Miss America*, subtitled *Teen Life*, which featured *Patsy Walker* and other comics. In 1946, it printed *Taffy*, a two page advice-for-teens column done in comic strip form by Phyllis Muchow. By 1947, the magazine had switched to *Rusty*, a similar strip drawn by a woman who signed her work only with her first name, Dottie.

The comic book industry, concerned with turning out comics quickly and cheaply, had evolved an assembly line process in which one person wrote the scripts, another illustrated them in pencil, another artist inked over the pencilled art, and a fourth did the lettering. Oddly, despite the long history of women writers and artists in the field, women inkers remain a rarity to this day. I have no idea why this particular part of the comic book process remains the last bastion of maleness.

However, there are and have been exceptions. In Lee's 1947 book, *Secrets Behind the Comics*, he refers to "Violet Barclay, glamorous girl inker of 'Rusty' and many other strips." Barclay, who later changed her first name to Valerie, was another woman who was heavily influ-

SO FAR WE HAVE FOLLOWED THE STRIP FROM THE TIME IT IS WRITTEN, TO THE PENCILLER, TO THE LETTERER!

Now, IT MUST GO TO STILL ANOTHER ARTIST FOR THE FINISHING TOUCH... IT MUST NOW GO TO *"THE INKER!"*

MEET VIOLET BARCLAY, GLAMOROUS GIRL INKER OF "RUSTY" AND MANY OTHER STRIPS...

As YOU CAN SEE, THERE ARE WOMEN ARTISTS AS WELL AS MEN IN THE COMIC MAGAZINE FIELD!

THE INKER IS THE ARTIST WHO INKS OVER THE PENCILLER'S DRAWINGS. BUT INSTEAD OF USING A PENCIL, THE INKER USES A PAINT BRUSH DIPPED INTO BLACK INDIA INK!

WANNA SEE WHAT "INKING" LOOKS LIKE?

31

Above: Page from *Secrets Behind the Comics*, by Stan Lee, introducing "Violet Barclay, glamorous girl inker," and explaining the inking process in comics, 1947.

Top right: Violet Barclay at 26, when she worked for Timely comics, and (bottom right) Valerie Barclay today.

enced by Nell Brinkley as a child. She never really liked working on the more cartoonish comics of the Stan Lee-Martin Goodman teen line, preferring romance comic books, for which she could draw beautiful women. Today she does fashion illustration for a New York City agency and paints portraits in the style of John Singer Sargent for her own enjoyment. Fittingly, she has also drawn a number of "pop art" ads in her old romance comics style.

Ann Brewster, one of the Fiction House artists, inked over the pencils of Robert H. Webb for the Classics Illustrated adaptation of *Frankenstein* and *Mr. Midshipman Easy*, as well as drawing

Left: *Spurned!* from *Complete Love Magazine*, 1954. Art by Valerie Barclay.

Below: Contemporary fashion drawing by Valerie Barclay.

for Classics Illustrated herself. Another woman who drew for Classics was Lillian Chestney. With a style much more closely related to fairy tale illustration than to comics, she was perfectly suited to adapt *Gulliver's Travels* and *Arabian Nights* into comic form. Back in 1937, Merna Gamble had adapted *A Tale of Two Cities* into comic book form, not for Classics, but for National Comics, which later became DC Comics.

Editors of the post-war years, who seemed to reject the idea of women drawing action strips, obviously found no fault with these artists drawing teenage comics. Another genre in which women appeared to be welcome was the burgeoning field of romance comics, which had started in

Summer Lifestyle, Valerie Barclay, 1987.

Above: *Arabian Nights,* (left) from *Classics Illustrated,* 1943; art by Lillian Chestney, and *A Tale of Two Cities,* (right) Merna Gamble, 1937.

1947. With few exceptions, the stories in these books were hackneyed and cliched, but the art was often stylish and elegant, allowing women artists to draw what they seem to prefer drawing: graceful closeups of women's faces. Ann Brewster, Ruth Atkinson and Valerie Barclay all found their niche in books with such titles as *Love Romances, Lover's Lane, Young Love,* and *Complete Love.*

If women cartoonists were still accepted in the more traditional teen and romance comics, one would expect to also find them in funny animal comics. However, research has uncovered few women working in that field. Dotty Keller drew funny animal strips for Timely Comics briefly during the war and Etta Parks drew *Red Rabbit,* a funny-animal parody of cowboy comic hero *Red Ryder,* from 1949-51. Now working under her married name of Etta Hulme, she draws editorial cartoons for the *Fort Worth Star-Telegram.* Hulme, who has worked in this field for twenty years, confesses to being at least "mildly offended" upon reading in a book about editorial cartooning, *The Ungentlemanly Art,* that there are no women editorial cartoonists.

In the mid-'50s, Christine Lyttle, then using her married name Christine Smith, applied for work at Western Printing and Lithography, the company that produced comics for both the Dell and Whitman publishing companies. After being told that Western didn't "hire girls," the company took her on to do erasures and corrections for six weeks before reluctantly allowing her to draw. During her years with Western, Lyttle wrote and drew novelty pages, comic pages and inside front and back covers for various comic books,

The Things They Whispered, from *Love Tales,* 1957. Art by Ann Brewster.

My Dearest Passenger, from *Lover's Lane,* 1949. Another unusual story illustrated by Ruth Atkinson. The female protagonists of these stories were usually secretaries or nurses, but in this case, she is a bus driver.

Right: *My Man–and My Sister!,* from *Love At First Sight,* 1953. Art by Alice Kirkpatrick. Another woman suffering from Male Pseudonym Syndrome, Kirkpatrick, when she signed her name, used the name "Kirk."

Opposite page–

Top: *Red Rabbit,* 1959, Etta Parks Hulme.

Bottom: Etta Hulme, editorial cartoon, *Fort Worth Star-Telegram,* 1990.

including *Roy Rogers, Little Lulu, Tarzan,* and such Walt Disney books as *Mickey Mouse Almanac, Silly Symphonies* and *The Sleeping Beauty.* During all these years, the only artistic credit she was ever given in print was in an *I Love Lucy* coloring book, which she drew in 1959.

Marie Severin, possibly this country's most respected woman super hero artist, has a similar recollection. During the same years Lyttle worked for Western, Severin's employer, EC Comics, was experiencing difficulties discussed in Chapter 6, and she knew it was time to look for other work. Severin had heard that Walt Disney Productions had offices in New York City, so she looked them up. At the front desk, a small man with a Disney moustache did not bother to look at her portfolio. Instead, he informed her that Disney didn't hire women. "No women? Not at all?" stammered the aghast artist, who had been used to more egalitarian treatment at EC. The little man replied, "Follow me, I'll show you." He led her to a huge room with orderly rows of desks. At each desk was a lamp, and under each lamp sat a man in a white shirt, drawing. "See?" said the little man. Severin realized that she wouldn't want to work at a place like that, anyway.

It goes without saying that all those white-shirted men working for Disney were *white*, white-shirted men. If, after the war, action-oriented comics became a male-only domain, all nationally syndicated comics were and had been a white-only domain. Only three African-American cartoonists had managed to break the color barrier in comics during the entire first half of the century, and they had all been men. It is safe, then, to assume that it never occurred to Jackie Ormes, an African-American woman, to attempt selling her comic strip, *Torchy Brown*, to any white-owned newspaper or syndicate. So, in 1937, *Torchy Brown in Dixie to Harlem* debuted in the black-owned *Pittsburgh Courier,* and was syndicated to fourteen other black newspapers around the coun-

Christine
Smith, from
*Dell Comic
Album*, Dec.-
Feb., 1959.

Left: Christine Smith, rough sketch for a rejected novelty page intended for a Disney comic book, 1959, along with a letter from the editor (right), explaining the reason for rejection.

Top: Christine Smith, from Western's house publication *The Westerner,* November, 1956. Smith is third from left, holding a coffee cup, facing front. She was the only woman artist at Western. All the others were secretaries.

Above: Christine Lyttle (Smith) today, an award-winning commercial artist. Photo by the artist's daughter, Christine Hope.

about a black maid, and *Patty Jo 'n' Ginger.* Patty Jo, her little girl heroine, was manufactured as a doll in the late '40s and early '50s, and is believed to be America's first black character doll. Then, in 1950, Torchy returned to the comics page of the *Courier* in *Torchy Brown's Heartbeats.* In the style of her popular white sister, *Brenda Starr,* the beautiful black heroine found herself lost in the jungles of Brazil, caught in the clutches of a boa constrictor, or on a tramp steamer, fighting off the advances of a villainous First Mate in the middle of a hurricane. Always she moved from love interest to love interest. Like so many other women cartoonists before her, Ormes included paper dolls on the Sunday page, "Torchy's Togs." But instead of a Mystery Man, Torchy Brown was more likely to fall in love with a jazz musician or a young black doctor struggling to keep his clinic together in the rural South. What kept *Torchy Brown* from being a black soap opera was Ormes' treatment of segregation, bigotry, and, in an age when ecology was a virtually unknown word, environmental pollution.

Jackie Ormes is believed to be the first (and until recently, the only) black woman to have her own syndicated comic strip, but at least one other black woman cartoonist has been found. During the 1950s, Doris McClarty drew the jivetalking *Fireball Freddy* for *Hep,* a black humor magazine based in Texas, and published by Sepia.

If the heroines of women-drawn strips could no longer be detectives, counterspies or aviatrixes, the more traditional jobs were still open to them. Included in the teen line written by Stan Lee were *Tessie the Typist* and *Nellie the Nurse,* and during the late '40s, Dorothy Bond syndicated a strip dedicated especially to secretaries, *Chlorine.* What Bond's work lacks in the way of art, it makes up for in sarcasm. Indeed, one can almost hear the lines of her long-suffering office worker read by actress Eve Arden.

By the 1950s, comics were no longer

try. The start of the strip found its young heroine leaving her farm in the South to find work in New York's famous Cotton Club. As the story proceeded, she encountered romance and danger in Harlem. In 1940, Ormes' strip went on a ten-year hiatus, during which time Ormes drew two single-panel cartoons—*Candy,*

limited to the funny pages of newspapers, or to the garishly colored pages of comic books. Fashion is a field that has always been open to women, and in the '50s, Edna Kaula drew *Sally,* a strip which ran in the trade publication, *Fabrics. Fabrics* had realized the potential of messages sent out in strip form, and comics had long been used to sell products from soap to soup. Throughout the '40s and '50s, Marge Henderson's *Little Lulu,* moonlighting from her monthly panel in *The Saturday Evening Post,* sold Kleenex in the Sunday comics section of national newspapers.

But surely one of the most unusual use of comics was the *Subway Sun,* which took the form of a single-sheet subway car poster, appearing in New York City's subways from 1935 to 1966. Originally drawn by Fred Cooper, the strip, which stressed good subway manners in comic form to millions of straphangers, was taken over in 1946 by his assistant, Amelia Opdyke

Above: *Torchy in Heartbeats,* circa 1950, Jackie Ormes. Twenty years before the ecology movement, a perfect description of industrial pollution.

Left: Jackie Ormes at 70.

Fireball Freddie! by Doris McClarty, from *Hep* magazine, 1955.

Chlorine, Dorothy Bond, 1947.

The Girl Friends, by "Ruthee," circa 1950s, a strip in the same sarcastic vein as *Chlorine.* The artist's last name is unknown.

Sally, drawn by Edna Kaula, 1958.

Above: *Little Lulu* Kleenex advertisement, Marge Henderson, 1946.

Right: *Little Lulu* as drawn by Christine Smith, the only other woman besides Marge Henderson to draw the corkscrew-haired moppet. A puzzle page from Marge's *Little Lulu and Tubby in Alaska*, Dell, 1959.

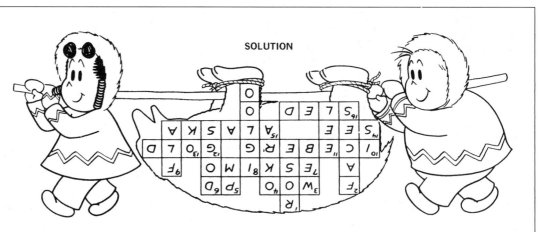

Jones, who signed her work "Oppy." Opdyke Jones, who also created Reddy Kilowatt, is credited with introducing the word "litterbug." Her first *Subway Sun* poster in 1946 was headlined "Nobody loves a litterbug." In a newspaper article from the 1960s she said, "Jitterbug was a popular expression at the time. I just changed the letter as part of a cleanup campaign." As is often the case when women cartoonists do not use obviously feminine names, most assumed Oppy to be a man. The newspaper article says, "Irate women would want to know who was this Mr. Oppy who depicted women inadvertently jabbing strangers with their

The Subway Sun, by "Oppy," circa 1960s.

umbrellas or clunking heads with hand-bags."

Teen comics and romance comics continued to employ women throughout the 1950s, but slowly the number of women in the field dropped. Some women, like Ruth Atkinson, left the industry for the traditional role of wife and mother, an action that was expected of young wives at the time. For others, like Valerie Barclay, "the bottom just dropped out." There was, indeed, a recession in the comics market during the late '50s, due in part to *Seduction of the Innocent,* a book written by Dr. Fredric Wertham in that decade, claiming that comics were responsible for juvenile delinquency. Although today his book is considered little more than a curiosity, he proved his point enough for the '50s mentality. *Seduction of the Innocent*

resulted in Senate hearings on comics and juvenile crime, the formation of a self-regulating Comics Code, and, eventually, the failure of most of the comic book publishing companies. As with any industry slump, many artists and writers were let go, and as with any industry, the first fired were women.

Patsy Walker comics died in 1967. *Millie the Model,* Stan Lee's favorite book in the teen line, hung on until 1974. By this time, neither book had been drawn by a woman for over twenty years. The two major comic book publishers that had survived the comics depression of the mid- to late 1950s were Marvel and DC, and both companies had, since the mid-'60s, been gearing themselves toward super heroes and the young boy market. Female-oriented comic books were slowly

Above: *Karen,* daily strip by Liz Berube, about 1968.

Left: *The Stranger Next Door,* from *Girl's Love,* 1970. Art by Liz Berube.

being phased out.

The last woman to illustrate a romance comic was Liz Berube, for DC's *Girl's Love,* and *Girl's Romances,* in the early 1970s. Berube had previously drawn, in her distinctive and decorative style, a syndicated strip called *Karen,* which ran in 40 newspapers. For the DC romance line she produced two love stories and many decorative single page fillers, such as horoscope pages. Her career with them lasted until the company ended their romance line in 1974.

At that time, there were exactly two women artists left working for mainstream comic books, but by then, young aspiring women cartoonists in America were turning their attention to a new kind of comic, one that seemed to hold more promise for their way of thinking, writing and drawing: the underground.

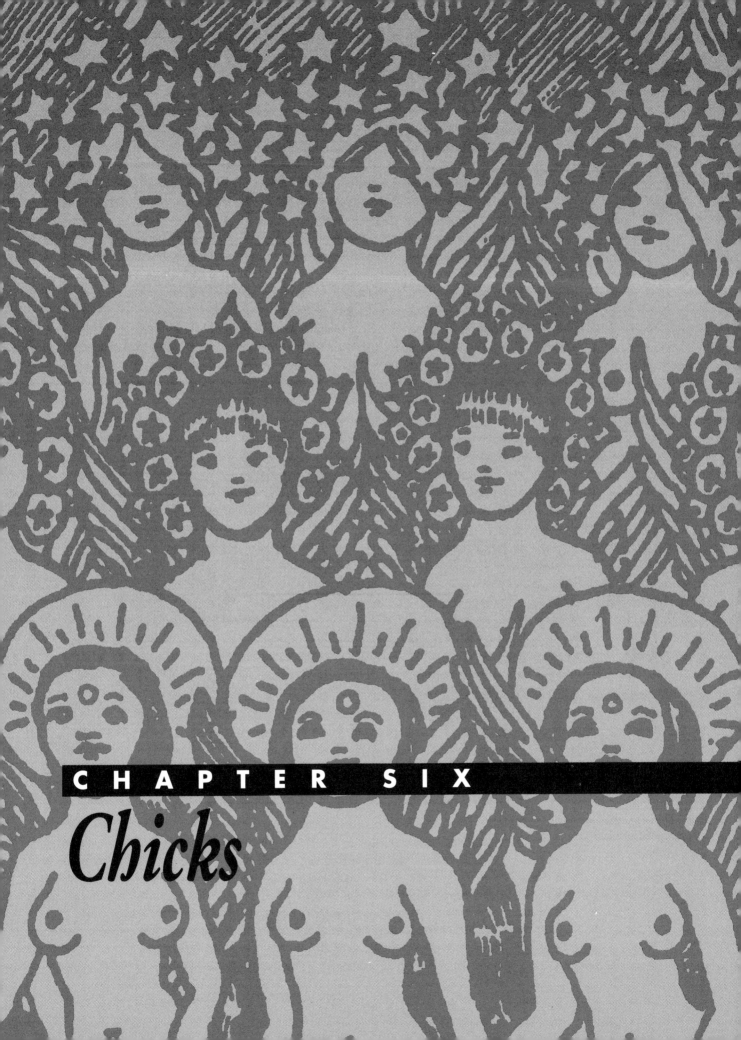

CHAPTER SIX

Chicks

CONFI - GIRL

EVERY SEPTEMBER AT HARVARD, THE SINS OF THE PAST YEAR ARE VISITED UPON EACH DESERVING PROFESSOR. WHETHER HE BE INSIPID, DISORGANIZED OR ILL-PREPARED, EACH IS GIVEN HIS DUE WHEN THE *CONFIDENTIAL GUIDE TO COLLEGE COURSES* HITS THE STANDS. FEW ESCAPE THE PUNGENT CRITI-CISM OF THEIR STUDENTS. THE ACID BARBS USUALLY INCLUDE SUCH APPRAISALS AS "VACUOUS," "EXECRABLE," "ABOMINABLE," "SHOULD TAKE A TEN-YEAR SABBATICAL." A BAD REVIEW INEVITABLY MEANS A DROP IN STUDENT ENROLLMENT FOR THE COURSE! AND THIS YEAR *THE POWERFUL MANTLE OF EDITOR FALLS TO RADCLIFFE JUNIOR LINDA GREENHOUSE.* SHE'LL GET $250 FOR EDITING WITH POISONED PEN.

SYLPH OF THE SEVENTH CRISIS

WHISPER HAD IT THAT LAWYER RICHARD NIXON WOULD BE GIVEN AN HONORARY DEGREE AT THE UNIVERSITY OF ROCHESTER! THAT FOE OF ACADEMIC FREEDOM? HAD HE NOT JOINED THE ONSLAUGHT AGAINST PRO-VIETCONGIST PROFESSOR GENOVESE? YES, INDEED! *JUNIOR MARJORIE McDIARMID, NEWSPAPER EDITOR, LED THE FRAY TO DENY NIXON THE DEGREE AT ANY COST!* OTHERS EAGERLY JOINED HER. THE SENIOR CLASS GOT UP A DEFIANT PETITION! A REFERENDUM WAS CALLED FOR. A SIT-IN WAS SCHEDULED. *WAIT A MINIT!* NIXON, PANIC-STRICKEN, ANNOUNCED HE WOULDN'T ACCEPT A DEGREE ANYWAY! SUCCESS. BUT HE *WOULD* SPEAK AT COMMENCEMENT... ON THE SUBJECT OF ACADEMIC FREEDOM. ONE LARGE HELPING OF CROW COMING UP!

THE FURTIVE PUSHER

WHILE CAMPUS COPS LOOK FOR HIM BEHIND BUSHES AND DEANS IMPLORE THE STUDENT BODY TO TELL THEM WHERE HE HANGS OUT, *THE CAMPUS PUSHER COOLLY OPER-ATES IN BROAD DAYLIGHT DOLING OUT SUGAR CUBES AND NICKEL BAGS AT A HEFTY PROFIT!* IN HARVARD SQUARE HIS NAME IS *HARRY*; AT BROADWAY AND 116TH STREET IT'S *JACK*. USUALLY AN INCONSPICU-OUS STUDENT IN SEMI-BEAT ATTIRE, THE PUSHER IS A FORBIDDEN TICKET TO EXPANDED CONSCIOUS-NESS ON CAMPUS AND A LINK WITH THE INTER-NATIONAL UNDERWORLD. BEWARE!

THE GOD OF FREE LOVE

EVEN AS THE FORCES OF HATE AND EVIL CONSPIRE TO ENGULF THE PLANET, *JEFFERSON POLAND, A JUNIOR AT MERRITT COLLEGE, CARRIES FOR-WARD THE NATIONWIDE STRUGGLE FOR UN-RESTRAINED LOVE!* CO-FOUNDER OF THE NEW YORK CITY LEAGUE FOR SEXUAL FREEDOM, EDITOR OF *INTERCOURSE*, PARTICIPANT IN A NUDE SWIM-IN, POLAND IS NOW TRYING TO FORCE COLLEGE HEALTH SERVICES TO COME ACROSS WITH CONTRACEPTIVE PILLS FOR WOMEN STUDENTS! IMPRESSED BY HIS CAMPAIGN, STUDENTS AT STANFORD HAVE ALREADY VOTED 2-1 IN FAVOR OF THE PILL! *VICTORY IS IN SIGHT!*

Drawings by Marie Severin

Marie Severin, illustrations for *Esquire* magazine, 1966

In 1953, EC Comics cartoonist John Severin got his kid sister Marie a job with the company. In a 1988 interview with Steve Ringgenberg, published in Russ Cochran's reprint of *Psychoanalysis* maga-zine (an EC title), Marie Severin described the work she was hired to do:

"...they needed a colorist, sort of like a girl Friday, and I did stuff like that. Mostly I was the colorist there and did some odd jobs." Marie Severin had come from a family in which literally everyone drew, and, as she said in the interview, "I just took it for granted that's what one did in this house, so I did."

She was not to find work at actually *drawing* comics, however, for another thirteen years. In 1955, when EC cut back its line, partially as a result of public and industry reaction to Dr. Fredric Wertham's *Seduction of the Innocent*, she went to work for the Stan Lee-edited Timely/Atlas comics line, doing the same kind of work she had done at EC. A year and a half later, Timely also cut back its line, a victim of the recession that affected the entire industry. Severin freelanced as a commercial artist until 1964, when she returned to work for Lee at what had now become Marvel Comics.

For two more years Marie Severin continued to do production work at Marvel. By 1966, the company, with its contemporary super hero concepts, was enjoying a new popularity among college students. Characters like the angst-ridden *Spider-Man*, or the psychedelic *Doctor Strange* had become pop art, and Marvel was suddenly "in" enough for *Esquire* magazine to feature it. None of Marvel's artists felt that the article was important enough to take time out from their regular work to illustrate, so the job of providing five pages of art went by default to Severin. In the

Above: Marie Severin, *Doctor Strange*, 1966

Left: Marie Severin, self-portrait, 1976

1988 interview, she related how this finally resulted in her getting work as an artist: "When Mr. [Martin] Goodman [the Marvel publisher] saw my stuff in *Esquire*, he said, 'Why is she in production? You have a drawer.' So Stan says, 'Would you like to draw? I need you, Steve Ditko left.' So, okay." Starting with *Doctor Strange*, Severin became the regular penciller on such titles as *King Kull*, *Sub-Mariner* and *The Cat*, also pencilling innumerable cov-

Above and opposite page: Marie Severin, Marvel superhero parodies done for the *Comic Book Price Guide*, circa 1980.

Ramona Fradon, splash pages from (left) *Aquaman,* **1961 and (right)** *Metamorpho,* **1965.**

ers, as well as inking and coloring other artists' stories. In recent years, most of her work has appeared in Marvel's lighter books, such as *Muppet Babies* and *Fraggle Rock*, which she says she enjoys more than the action/super hero books. Possibly Severin's most delightful work has been done for the company's parody titles, *Crazy* and *Not Brand Ecch!*

In contrast to Severin, Ramona Fradon, fresh out of art school in 1950, got the first comics illustration job she applied for. For almost ten years she drew *Aquaman* for DC Comics, going on to co-create the character Metamorpho for the company. Then in 1965, a year before Marie Severin started drawing for Marvel, Fradon took a seven year leave of absence to raise her daughter. Upon her return to DC, she worked on such titles as *Superman, Batman* and *Plastic Man*, until leaving in 1980 to take over Dale

Messick's *Brenda Starr* strip, upon the creator's retirement.

Fradon had never been totally enthusiastic about working in the male-directed super hero genre. In a 1988 interview with Andy Mangels in *Amazing Heroes* magazine, she describes her feelings: "I always felt rather strange, like a fish out of water or something. Here I was in a totally male-dominated field. I had a lot of trouble with the subject matter as well. I was really not interested in drawing super heroes—male fantasies, you know? People hitting each other or scheming to take over the world...Something that has always jarred my eyes is to see the kind of heaviness and ugliness about most [male] comic art. There's not much sweetness to it. It's the tradition...the look. That always troubled me."

Severin and Fradon possessed the (for women) unusual ability to draw muscular

Trina Robbins, *Kid Karma,* **from** *The East Village Other,* **1968**

super heroes and violent action, even though they didn't necessarily like what they were drawing. But what of the majority of women cartoonists, in a field that had converted almost entirely to the super hero genre? Carol Kalish, vice-president at Marvel comics, gave her opinion in an interview with Heidi MacDonald for the same issue of *Amazing Heroes* in which Fradon was interviewed:

> *Comic books now are mainly oriented towards boys; they mainly deal with boys' power fantasies, so they might not be very attractive to a female creator. It's not that you have to create books for women before you have female creators who could work in the industry. You also have to have a change in the attitudes of female creators...that this is a*

commercial operation, and that if they want to play in the comic book industry they're going to have to bend their creative talents...I've been in a lot of discussions with female creators who keep finding that their style of art isn't something that the comic book companies want to see. Instead of saying, well I can work in a variety of styles, they say, well, I don't want to work for you at all... We don't have a lot of female creators who are willing to compromise.

I suggest the possibility that most women cartoonists are not able to compromise, and although they may very well be able to work in a variety of styles, that variety rarely includes super heroes. Following are a series of quotes, all from the above mentioned issue of *Amazing*

129

Nancy Kalish, ("Panzika"), *Busy Boxes,* from *Gothic Blimp Works,* 1968

Kay Rudin, from *Yellow Dog*, 1968

Heroes, by some of the few women who can and do draw super hero comics today:

Mary Wilshire: *We* [women] *seem to be interested in telling different kinds of stories. I wish there wasn't so much obsession with violence...when it's gratuitously violent and horrible, it doesn't do anything for me.*

Cara Sherman-Tereno: *My experience has been that we don't see things quite the same way* [as male creators].

Cynthia Martin: *There are things that I can't stand drawing...I can't handle drawing guns or cars, or anything like that. I like to draw ballet and dancers, real life stuff...*

Colleen Doran: *If it offends me, I probably can't draw it!*

Luckily for many aspiring women cartoonists, at the same time that the kind of comics which most women could draw had all but vanished, a new kind of comic appeared on the cultural horizon. In 1965, I saw my first underground newspaper, *The East Village Other*, ("EVO") a counter culture tabloid from New York City. One of the pages was filled with a strange conglomeration of drawings, almost abstractly put together in loose panel form. It was not yet called by the name it would later earn from appearing in underground newspapers—underground comics (or "comix," as they were often called, to distinguish them from the super hero genre). The comic in *The East Village Other*, signed "Panzika," was called *Gentle's Tripout*, and was the first of its kind that I ever saw. I did not know at the time that "Panzika" was a woman, Nancy Kalish. I was, however, inspired to try producing some of my own strips, and by

Willy Mendes, from *Illuminations*, 1971

Julie Wood ("Jewelie Goodvibes"), from *All Girl Thrills*, 1970 (left), and Nan Pettit, from *Illuminations*, 1971 (right).

1966 I, too, was being published sporadically in EVO. Two years later, Kalish and I were joined by Willy Mendes on the pages of *Gothic Blimp Works*, a comic tabloid published by EVO. At the same time, in Berkeley, the fanciful work of Kay Rudin, who had left a job drawing greeting cards in Ohio, was being published in another comic tabloid, *Yellow Dog*.

The comics these women drew were as different from the comics being published by Marvel or DC—or most comics published today in the alternative comics industry—as a tie-dyed T-shirt is from a business suit. The word that best describes early underground comix is psychedelic. Plot was not considered important. One got the impression that if the reader got stoned enough on controlled substances, he or she would understand the comic—or at least think so. The underground artist, more concerned with design than content, simply put felt-tipped pen to paper and let it flow, man.

During the years that these women were doing their own thing, college student Lee Marrs was working part-time as assistant to *Little Orphan Annie* cartoonist Tex Blaisdell, and contributing gags to the syndicated strip *Hi & Lois*. By late 1969, Marrs, Robbins and Mendes converged in San Francisco, and Marrs discovered the Underground. "I didn't know they existed until I moved [to San Francisco]," she said in an interview. "The things that were being done were so

Suzanna Lasker ("Suzu"), *Housewife vs. Hippie,* **for Alternative Features Services, early 1970s**

much more exciting and interesting [than what was being done at Marvel and DC]."

In 1971, along with John Berger and Mal Warwick, Marrs formed the Alternative Features Service (AFS), which distributed news, features and comics mainly to college and underground newspapers. The woman cartoonists distributed by the syndicate during its more than six-year existence included Marrs, Trina Robbins, Shelby Sampson, Bulbul, and Suzanna Lasker, who signed her name "Suzu."

When it came to comic books, however, Marrs "ran into another version of the closed system...in the Underground...It was kind of like a boy's club...a closed club...There was no way a beginning artist could break in, no place for it. All the underground comics consisted of friends printing friends. They were all buddies; they didn't even let us in."

Willy Mendes and I had made the same discovery, and we reacted to exclusion by producing our own comic books. In 1970, I had joined the staff of *It Ain't Me, Babe*, California's first feminist underground newspaper, and we soon produced *It Ain't Me, Babe* comics, the first all-woman comic book. Later in 1970, I put together *All Girl Thrills*, which included the work of Mendes and Julie Wood, who signed herself "Jewelie Goodvibes."

Above: Psychedelia gives way to politics. Art by the It Ain't Me, Babe Collective for *It Ain't Me, Babe* comics, 1970.

Right: The It Ain't Me, Babe Collective. Left to right: Meredith Kurtzman (in oval), Carole (last name unknown), Trina Robbins (with Casey Robbins), Peggy (last name unknown), Lisa Lyons, Michele Brand, Willy Mendes, Hurricane Nancy Kalish ("Panzika").

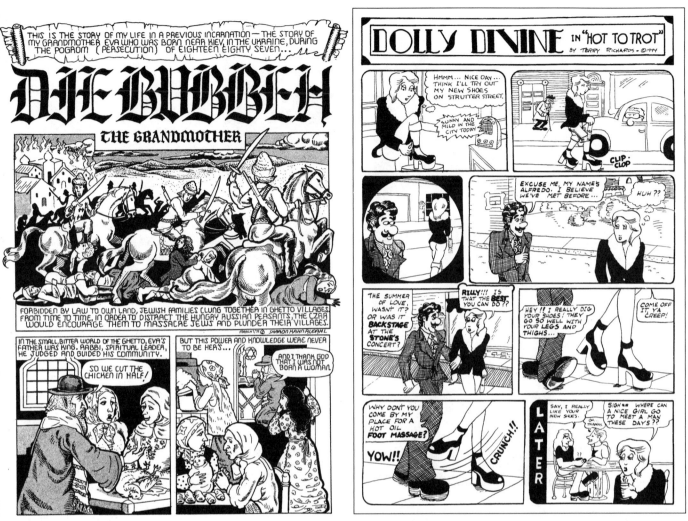

Sharon Rudahl, *Die Bubbeh,* from *Wimmen's Comix,* 1975 (left) and Terre Richards, *Dolly Divine,* from *Wimmen's Comix,* 1974.

1971 saw the publication of Mendes' *Illuminations,* which featured psychedelic comic pages by Nan Pettit, as well as by Goodvibes and myself.

In 1972, Sharon Rudahl, fresh from Madison, Wisconsin where she had been drawing political comics for the local underground paper, *Takeover,* was living at the San Francisco Good Times commune, and working on their underground paper. Terre Richards, who had come to San Francisco in 1969 from Pennsylvania, was working for *It Ain't Me, Babe* comic book publisher Ron Turner. Lee Marrs, who had found out about *It Aint Me, Babe* too late to be included in the book, was working on her own comic, *Pudge, Girl Blimp,* which would not see print for two more years. *It Aint Me, Babe* had sold well

enough for Turner to decide to put out an ongoing women's comic book. In a 1979 interview in *Cultural Correspondence* magazine, Richards told about the formation of this new book:

> *...I was looking for a more creative outlet, one that would incorporate a growing interest in writing and animation... As a result of the Women's Movement there was a growing awareness of women in all areas of the arts as well as a newly developing market for women's work in publishing, so the time was right for an all-woman's comic, and when I heard from my boss...that Pat Moodian was editing a women's comic and they were looking for contributors, I jumped at the chance...Thus,*

Left: The Wimmen's Comix Collective, 1972. Left to right: Michele Brand, Lee Marrs, Lora Fountain, Pat Moodian (editor), Sharon Rudahl, Shelby Sampson, Aline Kominsky, Trina Robbins, Karen Marie Haskell, Janet Wolfe Stanley. Self-portraits by the various artists.

Below: Lee Marrs, *Cyberfenetics*, from *Wimmen's Comix*, 1974

Wimmen's Comix *was born.*

Moodian, Richards, Robbins, Rudahl, and Marrs joined with Michelle Brand, Lora Fountain, Shelby Sampson, Aline Kominsky, Karen Marie Haskell, and Janet Wolfe Stanley to produce the first ongoing all-woman comic book, which survives to this day. Influenced by the political consciousness of the early '70s, in which many underground newspapers were being manufactured collectively, the founders of *Wimmen's* put their book together in a way in which no male-produced comics, underground or otherwise, had been done. Richards, from the same interview:

> *We...decided that...we would produce an on-going title of comics by women and that we would function as a collective, a term used rather loosely in those days to mean there would be no leader or editor, but instead a rotating editorship, with everyone contributing their energy to the paperwork and general supportiveness of the group.*

Another title beat *Wimmen's Comix* to the comic book stores by two months.

Tits'n'Clits was the work of two Southern California women, Joyce Farmer and Lynn Chevely (under the pseudonym "Chin Lyvely"), who had formed their own publishing company, Nannygoat Productions, as a reaction to the sexism they were seeing in male-produced underground comics. Interviewed in *Cultural Correspondence*, Chevely talked about the creation of the title, which has always dealt with sex from a woman's point of view:

> *The decision to be vulgar rather than high class arose out of sheer ignorance. Neither of us was much of a comics fan, but at the time we started I owned a bookstore, sold u.g.s [undergrounds], and was impressed by their*

honesty but loathed their macho depiction of sex. Our work, originally, was a reaction to the glut of testosterone in comics... As most of us know, sex is a very political business. All we want to do is equalize that by telling our side... Our original commitment was to concentrate on female sexuality, and our titles indicate that.

In 1973, struggling fine artist Melinda Gebbie discovered *Wimmen's Comix*. In a 1980 interview with me, she talked about her experience:

> *...I went to the Hall of Flowers, in Golden Gate Park. It was a publisher's fair. Lee Marrs was sitting at a booth and I got very interested in hearing*

Top left: Lyn Chevely ("Chin Lyvely") "concentrates on female sexuality" in *Those Perfectly Permeable Peters Sisters*, from *Tits'n'Clits*, 1973.

Above: Art by Joyce Farmer, story by Lyn Chevely, *Silver Clouds are Sometimes Lined With Hot Air*, from *Tits'n'Clits*, 1977.

Melinda Gebbie, signing her work "Clothilde," deals with sexual confusion in her first comic for *Wimmen's, Super Cilia,* 1973.

Roberta Gregory, *A Modern Romance,* from *Wimmen's Comix,* 1974.

Above: Wimmen just wanna have fun: the Wimmen's Comix Collective at a 1975 gallery exhibit of their work. Standing, left to right: Becky Wilson, Trina Robbins, Shelby Sampson, Ron Turner (publisher), Barb Brown, Dot Bucher. Sitting: Melinda Gebbie, Lee Marrs.

Left: Political, but still psychedelic: art by Barbara "Willy" Mendes, drawn during the Persian Gulf War, 1991.

about women's comics so she told me to come to the next meeting. They put out two issues and I ended up being in issue number three... And they told me I could do what I wanted, so when I went home I thought, "Now what am I gonna do?" I'd never drawn anything in windows before, and the only thing that I could think of, to draw with any kind of sincerity, since I'd never been into fuzzy animals or jokes, that I'd draw something about my sexual confusion...it was mostly the fact that I was a woman that...made my story valid.

In 1974 Roberta Gregory, the first published lesbian comic artist, was introduced in the pages of *Wimmen's*. In *Cultural Correspondence* she says: "The thing that got my first story in print was seeing the virtually straight *Wimmen's Comix* #1...and I thought, hey, what's going on? So I wrote a lesbian story...it

didn't turn out quite like I wanted it to, but at least it was a valid place to be coming from."

Each issue of *Wimmen's* and *Tits'n'Clits* included new women. Not all of them remained with the books. By 1972, Willy Mendes, one of the earliest and most enthusiastic of the women underground cartoonists, had moved to Southern California, where today she runs the Los Angeles-based Barbara Mendes gallery. But by the end of the decade, most of the regular contributors had produced at least one comic book of their own. More women were finding in underground comics an opportunity which no longer existed in the super hero mainstream comics industry. Lee Marrs speaks for the majority of women cartoonists in the '70s when she says, "It was really the *Wimmen's Comix* group, since that was a place to get encouragement and stuff, that kept me going."

CHAPTER SEVEN

Women, Womyn, Wimmin

Roberta Gregory delineates the average woman's experience in a comic book store. From *Naughty Bits.*

ALL WOMEN'S DIALOGUE INSPIRED BY OR TAKEN DIRECTLY FROM ACTUAL CONVERSATIONS WITH AUTHOR

I magine walking into a bookstore, hoping to find a good mystery or historical novel, and discovering that the store carries nothing but Westerns. Upon inquiry, a clerk points out that they do actually carry some mysteries, but those few he shows you, crowded on a bottom shelf together with the other non-Western titles, are printed on cheap paper without color covers. The bookstore is out of the particular mystery you want, the clerk informs you. They only ordered two copies of it, he adds, because, as everyone knows, mystery book readers don't go into bookstores. Of course, logic tells you, mystery book readers *won't* go into bookstores that carry only Westerns.

For roughly twenty years, this has been the situation in American comic book stores. Most people over the age of forty remember buying comic books at a drugstore or candy store, but since the 1970s, most comic books have been sold only in comic book stores. While there are exceptions, the majority of comic book stores tend to carry super hero comics by the major comic publishers, Marvel and DC, with a smaller stock of super hero comics produced by independent publishers. Some of these stores may grudgingly display a few underground or experimental comics, many of which include women among their contributors. The stores are even more grudging about stocking the miniscule number of comic books which specifically appeal to women or young girls, rightfully reasoning that girls and women don't come into comic book stores. The reason why? Mystery readers won't bother coming into a store that stocks only Westerns.

In today's comic book industry, the majority of women cartoonists are pub-

Some women cartoonists from *Drawn and Quarterly:* Top, Anne Bernstein; Middle, Carol Swain and Ida Marx; Bottom, Fiona Smyth.

lished in underground, or experimental, comic books from small companies. This is another way or saying that the majority of today's women cartoonists do not earn a living drawing comics. For the most part, underground rates for a finished, pencilled and inked page range from a low of $25 to a high of $75. Compare this to DC and Marvel comics' starting rates for a finished scripted, pencilled, inked and lettered page of about $235. (This does not include payment to the colorist, since the average underground or small independent comic is black and white.)

Above: A sampling of lesbian cartoonists: Top, Jackie Urbanovic and Mary Wings; Middle, Joan Hilty and Leslie Ewing. All from *Gay Comix*. Bottom, Cheela Smith, from *Girljock*.

Right: Gay and lesbian cartoonists gathered in New York in 1991 for a cartoon exhibit at The Lesbian and Gay Community Services Center. Standing, left to right: Howard Cruse, the most well known gay cartoonist in the United States, and first editor of *Gay Comix*; Jennifer Camper; Ivan Velez, creator of *Tales From the Closet*, a comic book series aimed at gay and lesbian teenagers; Jackie Urbanovic. Seated: left, Alison Bechdel; right, Andrea Natalie.

One extremely prestigious comic title, until recently, did not pay its artists and writers anything at all, theorizing that the honor of being published in the book was worth more than mere money. Contributors were paid in free copies. The underground comic publishers are not necessarily to be faulted for their low rates. Print runs can be as low as 2,000, and an underground comic is considered a great success if it sells 10,000 copies. Compare this to a DC comics print run of 100,000. In that alternate universe in which bookstores carry only Westerns, those few publishers of mysteries would also pay their writers very little, because of the low print run of the books.

Some of the many underground or independent comic book anthologies that number women cartoonists among their contributors are the now defunct *Centrifugal Bumble Puppy* and *Prime Cuts*, from Fantagraphics; Canada's *Drawn and Quarterly*; *Raw* magazine; *Gay Comix*, which includes many lesbian contributors; and *Ripoff Comix*, published by Rip Off Press. Anthology comics which print either all women or a majority of women cartoonists include Last Gasp's *Weirdo*, especially under the editorship of Aline Kominsky-Crumb; *Real Girl*, published by Fantagraphics, and *Tits'n'Clits* and

Mary Fleener discusses *Tits'n'Clits* with her mother. From *Weirdo*.

Some Women cartoonists from *Weirdo:* Top, editor Aline Kominsky-Crumb and Diane Noomin; Middle, Linda Crothers; Bottom, Penny Moran and Carol Tyler.

Above: *Tits'n'Clits* co-publisher Joyce Farmer tells about the formation of her controversial comic book in a story in *Itchy Planet.* The two women in the strip are Farmer (long hair) and co-founder Lynn Chevely (short hair).

Right: A sampling from a decade of *Wimmin's Comix.* Top, Suzy Varty; middle, Leslie Sternbergh; bottom, left to right, Joey Epstein, Julie Hollings ("Jewels"), Trina Robbins.

Wimmin's Comix, both of which have survived from the 1970s. (In 1992, with issue #17, *Wimmen's Comix* officially removed the "men" from its name and became *Wimmin's Comix.*)

At the time of this writing, many of the women cartoonists published in the above titles have come out with one or more of their own solo books. Some of these are Carol Lay's *Good Girls,* Julie Doucet's *Dirty Plotte,* Roberta Gregory's *Naughty Bits,* Krystyne Kryttre's *Death Warmed Over,* the late Dori Seda's *Lonely Nights,* Mary Fleener's *Slutburger,* and Aline Kominsky-Crumb's *Power-Pak.*

The past ten years have seen the rise of comic books with specialized themes. *World War 3*, a political

More from *Wimmin's Comix*: Top, Sharon Rudahl; long panel on the left, Cecelia Capuana; upper middle panel, Myra Hancock, lower middle, left to right, Susan Catherine, Jackie Urbanovic; bottom, Phoebe Gloeckner.

Still more from *Wimmin's Comix*: top, Lee Binswanger; bottom, Judy Becker, left, and Lee Marrs.

comic magazine, featuring feminist and other left-of-liberal comics, includes a good number of women, and devoted a recent issue to the problems of sexism. Many lesbian comic books and magazines can now be found in gay or women's book stores, as well as in the more open-minded comic book stores. One of the most successful of these books, *Girljock*, features what may be the most specialized subject in the comics industry—sports comics by lesbian cartoonists.

Another recent specialization in the field is the benefit comic book, inspired by the benefit rock concerts of the past ten years. In two of these books, half or more of the contributors were women: *Choices,* a pro-choice benefit book for the National Organization of Women; and *Strip AIDS USA*, a benefit for the Shanti Project. *Strip AIDS USA* included all the gay and lesbian cartoonists the editors could contact, something one would expect from editors putting together a book about AIDS. Yet, a 1989 British comic book about homophobia actually

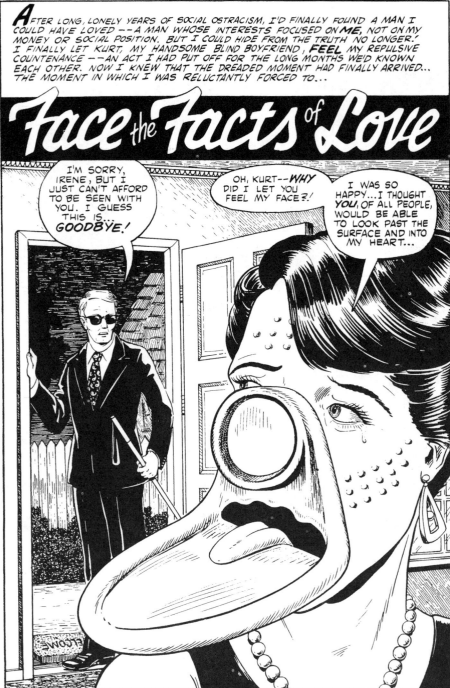

Above: *Good Girls,* Carol Lay's satire on the romance genre.

Top right: Myra Hancock (left), British cartoonist who appeared in *Wimmen's Comix* in 1985, and Lora Fountain (right), who was in *Wimmen's Comix* in 1972, get together at a comic convention in Lucca, Italy, in 1984.

Shary Flenniken was cartoon editor, printed many cartoons by women and became a showcase for new women cartoonists, such as Holly K. Tuttle and Mimi Pond, whose hilarious comic strip is now carried on the back page of *Seventeen* magazine. Not all women's or girl's magazines have been as conscientious. In its earliest issues, *MS* magazine ran a regular strip called *Mary Selfworth*, which was credited to "Vincenza Colletta," although the editors knew the artist was actually Marvel cartoonist Vince Colletta.

There is a blurred line between independent comic book publishers and underground publishers. For clarity's sake, I have chosen to define "undergrounds" as the more experimental titles, and "independent" as those publishers which, though smaller than Marvel and DC, publish mostly super hero and adventure titles. Many independent publishers do

contained few homosexual contributors.

Some magazines also carry or have carried comics. The now defunct *National Lampoon,* especially during the years that

From *Dirty Plotte*,
1991. Cartoonist Julie
Doucet cracks herself
up.

Top: From *Desert Peach,* Donna Barr's solo book about Rommel's little-known gay younger brother.

Right: Krystyne Kryttre, from *Weirdo.*

not have a great track record of employing women cartoonists, but there are notable exceptions. Chief of these is WaRP Graphics, run by cartoonist Wendy Pini and her writer husband, Richard. After the Pinis tried unsuccessfully to sell their comic concept, *Elfquest,* to every major publisher, they formed WaRP Graphics and self-published what became one of the most successful black and white comic series of the 1980s, and one of the most popular among female readers. Ironically, Marvel Comics, which had rejected *Elfquest,* eventually reprinted it in color under the Marvel logo. WaRP Graphics has since expanded to publish work by other writers and cartoonists. They were the first publishers of Colleen Doran's *A Distant Soil,* a concept the artist created at the age of twelve. Doran continues to write and draw *A Distant Soil,* which is now regularly published by Aria Press, and she also draws for both Marvel and DC Comics.

Eclipse Comics has published comic books by Leila Dowling, Lea Hernandez, Cynthia Martin, Donna Barr, and Trina Robbins. In 1985, they published the now out-of-print *Women and the Comics,* the first book about women in the comics industry, co-writ-

In *Lonely Nights*, 1986, Dori Seda's only solo book, the artist gives the reader a glimpse into her night life. Seda's untimely death in 1988 at the age of 36 turned her into a cult figure in the world of underground comics.

153

Above: A panel on women in comics at the 1986 San Diego comic convention. Left to right: Karen Berger, editor, DC Comics; Roberta Gregory; Carol Kalish, vice president, Marvel Comics; Lee Binswanger; Leslie Sternbergh.

Right: *The Lost Girls,* drawn by Melinda Gebbie and written by Alan Moore, 1992. From *Taboo,* published by Tundra.

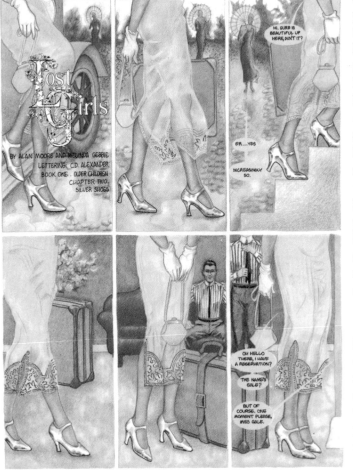

ten by myself and Eclipse editor Catherine Yronwode.

Also noteworthy is Renegade Press, run by Deni Loubert, the only woman publisher in the independents. For a two-year period, until its dissolution, Renegade published *Wimmin's Comix,* and also attempted to bring back the romance genre with two issues of *Renegade Romance,* an anthology comic book which included both male and female cartoonists.

As shown, those cartoonists working for either Marvel or DC can earn a very good living. However, a study of three months' worth of Marvel comics turned up sixty-two male pencillers, and five female pencillers. The ratio of inkers is more extreme: during those three months, Marvel comics employed exactly two women inkers. The representation of women cartoonists at DC is similar. As noted in the previous chapter, very few women draw in the style that is currently accepted by all companies that publish action/super hero titles. This is also true in England. In an article about the British comic market published in *The Comics Journal,* Nick Hasted wrote about *Ceasefire,* a British all-woman anti-war comic book, published by Knockabout Press to rave reviews: "When I showed *Ceasefire* to both editors [of Fleetway, the major British publisher of action/super hero comic books], they rejected almost all of its contributors. 'I can't see any of that going into *2000 AD* [Fleetway's best selling title].'"

Men in the comic book industry, both professionally or as comic fans, seem to have reservations about women's art. At a recent comic convention, Linda Medley, a cartoonist whose work has appeared in independently published

Top: From Molly Kiely's adaptation of the Marquis De Sade's *Philosophy in the Bedroom,* published by Wooley Comix, 1992.

Left: Some women cartoonists from *World War 3*: top, Irene Ledwith; middle, Villa Piazza; bottom, and Sabrina Jones, Kathryn Hyatt, 1992.

Kris Kovick, from *Girljock*, 1992

From *Choices*, 1990; two different visions of choice. Top, Alison Bechdel, *Dykes to Watch Out For*; bottom, Bulbul.

From the pages of *National Lampoon*: top to bottom, Shary Flenniken, Mimi Pond, Roz Chast.

Above: *Aunt Mary's Kitchen,* by M.K. Brown, from *National Lampoon.*

Left: Holly K. Tuttle, who started in *National Lampoon.* This strip is from *Real Stuff,* published by Fantagraphics.

Elfquest, by Wendy and Richard Pini, 1992

A Distant Soil, by Coleen Doran, 1992

Above: Coleen Doran

Top: June Brigman

Above: Wendy and Richard Pini

Left: Ramona Fradon. These three photos were taken by Mary Wilshire during a women cartoonists show at the Museum of Cartoon Art, Port Chester, New York, 1984.

Above: *Weasel Attack!,* by Leila Dowling, published by Eclipse.

Left: *Batman,* drawn by Mary Mitchell, inked by Bruce Patterson. DC Comics, 1992.

comic books as well as DC Comics, sat at a table displaying her original comic pages for sale. For most of the day, people passed by without looking at her work. Finally she asked her brother to man her table while she took a two hour break. Upon her return, she learned that her brother had sold a number of her pages. People passing the table had noticed that the name on his convention badge was the same as the name on the comic pages, and assumed he was the artist. When they had seen the real artist sitting behind the table, they had either decided that because she was a woman she could not be the artist, or that because the art was by a woman, they would not like it.

Yet, in the earlier part of this century, men and women drew successful comics in an immense variety of styles.

Twenty-five years after the publication death of typical teenager *Patsy Walker* (in the '70s, there was an attempt made to turn her into a super heroine named *Hellcat,* but the less said of that, the better), Marvel publishes two regular comic books for young girls, two *Barbie* titles, and another, Barbara Slate's *Sweet XVI,* irregularly. DC, after a brief attempt at the young girl market in 1987, with *Angel Love,* also by Barbara Slate, now publishes none. Proposals for comics aimed at young girls (or women) are discouraged at both companies, because "girls (or women) don't read comics." This is, of course, true in an age when comic book stores don't offer anything for young girls or women. Yet we know it has not always

been true.

Women cartoonists will not be able to earn a living wage drawing for comic books until the major comic publishers return once again to the great variety of comics they published thirty years ago, and until the comic book stores open their shelves to a diversity of titles and cartooning styles. Obviously, the vast amount of men who draw for underground and independent comic publishers, in a style other than super heroic, would also benefit from such a change.

Archie Comics should be applauded for continuing to publish the adventures of *Betty, Veronica, Jughead* and the gang. Along with *Barbie,* these are the only comics that currently appeal specifically to young girls. Archie Comics, a much smaller company than Marvel or DC, has employed a few women cartoonists off and on throughout the past ten years.

Marvel and DC each have one title on which they employ or have employed a good number of women, both writers and artists. At DC comics that book is *Wonder Woman.* Originally created by psychologist William Moulton Marston in 1940, and intended from the first to appeal to girls, the story of the Amazon princess has indeed, for fifty years, been a "girl's book." However, for its first forty-six years,

Above: From *Galactic Girl Guides,* written by Elaine Lee and drawn by Linda Medley.

Top: *Spider-Man,* drawn by Paty Cochrum, for Marvel Comics, 1985.

Attempts made over the past decade to bring back teen comics for young girls: Top, left to right, *Angel Love,* by Barbara Slate; *Meet Misty,* by Trina Robbins. Bottom, left to right, *Vickie Valentine,* drawn by Barb Rausch from a script by *Katy Keene* artist/creator Bill Woggon; *California Girls* by Trina Robbins. Although all of these titles received excellent reader response, they were not carried in enough numbers by the comic book stores, and so did not survive. All three women are currently working on *Barbie.*

the book was drawn and written exclusively by men. Finally, in 1986, I was hired to draw a four part *Wonder Woman* miniseries, *The Legend of Wonder Woman.* Shortly after the mini-series, Mindy Newell became one of the writers of the newly revamped book, and in 1989, DC produced a special *Wonder Woman* annual which was illustrated by ten women cartoonists. After the annual, Cynthia Martin drew one special issue, and then the book was taken over by Jill Thompson, who became its artist until 1992, when she moved on to another title.

Marvel's "girl's book" is *Barbie.* Two titles, *Barbie* and *Barbie Fashion,* both

Women cartoonists who have worked for Archie Comics over the past ten years: top, Kathleen Webb, from *Betty and Veronica*; bottom, left to right, Lori Walls, from *Marvelous Maureen*; Amanda Connor, from *Bayou Billy*.

Women draw *Barbie*. Top row: Mary Wilshire and June Brigman. Middle row: Amanda Connor, Anna Maria Cool. Bottom: Barb Rausch. Wilshire, Connor and Cool are inked by Trina Robbins; Brigman and Rausch are inked by John Lucas, who drew *Katy Keene* for Archie Comics after the Bill Woggon creation was revived.

Women cartoonists draw *Wonder Woman*.

Opposite page: top row, left to right: Trina Robbins, Jan Dursema, Barb Rausch. Bottom row, left to right: Cara Sherman, inked by Leslie Sternbergh, Jill Thompson.

This page, top to bottom: Cynthia Martin, Ramona Fradon, Carol Lay; bottom row, left to right: Mary Wilshire, Colleen Doran.

Above: Another view of *Wonder Woman*, by Carol Moiseiwitsch, 1985.

Below: *Barbie* artist Anna Maria Cool, at a 1992 signing at Oak Leaf Comics, in Mason City, Iowa.
Photo by Andy Cool.

based on the adventures of this century's most loved and hated doll, are published monthly by the company. The stories are written by three women: Barbara Slate, Lisa Trusiani, and Trina Robbins, and is drawn by six different women.

In a letter to me, a male editor at DC Comics had this to say about one of the best *Barbie* artists: "[the artist] has a clean, designy style, but it's not right (to my mind) for engaging comic strip narrative...the range of expression is very limited, and there's not much variety of views (the 'camera' is generally parallel to the plane of action and placed at eye level). There's no variety of moods."

One is reminded of the editors at England's *2000 AD* rejecting the contributors to the all-woman *Ceasefire*. For "limited expression" and "no variety of moods," read "the characters do not snarl, bellow in rage, or grimace with pain." For "not much variety of views," read "there is no forced extreme perspective, bird's eye views or worm's eye views," all of which, although they have no real artistic reason, are part of the current action/super hero esthetic. The male editor knows what young boys like, but has no concept of what girls like.

We know about much of the sexism that affected women cartoonists in the past: the blackballing of Hilda Terry by the NCS in 1950, women artists who changed their names because they felt boys would not read comics signed by a woman. What we may never know is whether any of these women were forced to endure sexual harassment. Only recently has the public become more aware of the extent of sexual harassment in almost every industry, and the comics field is no exception. Industry horror stories range from overt harassment (male editors and artists asking women cartoonists to sit on their laps or kiss them) to the telling of sexist jokes in the workplace (when one woman cartoonist objected to a male cartoonist telling rape jokes, he answered, "Aw, come on, I'm just trying to get a rise out of you!"), to one comic book publisher holding an anniversary celebration for his company, to which he invited male and female contributors, at an "adult" theater that featured stripping and live sex shows.

A woman comic artist told this story to me:

A publisher with the power to hire and fire wanted to know if I would be interested in doing some work for his company. As it was early in my career, I was ecstatic at the opportunity. He then asked if I would like to accompany him to a banquet where he would introduce me to some of the industry's powers-that-be and discuss some projects over our meal. Again I greeted the idea with enthusiasm. His next question, or should I say request, took me totally off-guard. If I was to accompany him in public, would I please wear an above-the-knee skirt and high heels? Much to my discredit and discomfort I complied with his request and left the banquet later feeling less an artist and more a piece of artwork. The only upside to this fiasco was that I did indeed receive work from his company, which in turn led to bigger and better projects.

Barb Kaalberg, one of the few women inkers in the field, told of sitting at her

Above: From *Yuppies From Hell*, by Barbara Slate, 1991. This trade paperback, aimed at a female audience, could be considered Marvel Comics' most unusual title. Printed in black and white, and carried in bookstores, it bears no resemblance to Marvel's super hero books, yet it has sold well enough for two editions to be produced.

Barbara Slate, from the back cover of *Yuppies From Hell*.
Photo by Bert Stern.

Self-syndicated cartoonist Nina Paley comments on a nationally syndicated strip, 1992.

publisher's table during a trade show, when she was approached by a comics dealer. "He began uttering a few flowery comments that soon turned suggestive. He leaned a little closer and abruptly declared: 'You'd better be real nice to me. I sell your books.'"

Compared to comic books, the world of newspaper strips is on another planet. One self-syndicated woman cartoonist defines comic books as "comics," and newspaper strips as "cartoons," thereby separating the worlds in her mind. Having already decided on my own definition in the introduction to this book, I will continue to call both industries "comics."

The benefit of newspaper strips for women cartoonists is obvious: Women *do* read newspapers. There are also drawbacks: It is difficult to get accepted by the large syndicates, which often have their

own prejudices against or for certain styles. Once accepted, the artist must usually sign away the rights to her comic creation. She is at the mercy of the syndicate, which can tell the artist what or what not to say or draw, and can fire her and hire someone else to take over the strip which she had originally created.

An option that hardly existed twenty years ago, yet is probably the best deal for women cartoonists today, is self-syndication. By the mid-'70s, the underground papers of the 1960s had evolved into something known as "the alternative weekly," a free tabloid, usually paid for by ads from local merchants. Most large American cities and college towns have at least one weekly newspaper. These papers are often given away in local bookstores and coffee houses, attracting a more bohemian or intellectual readership than the average daily. These readers demand

Above: The two most well-known self-syndicated women cartoonists. Top, Nicole Hollander; bottom, Lynda Barry.

Right: *Ask Aunt Violet,* by Caryn Leschen, from the *San Francisco Weekly,* 1992.

comic strips which are more challenging than those found in the dailies. Among the many cartoonists who meet that demand are Lynda Barry with *Ernie Pook's Comeek,* Nicole Hollander with *Sylvia,* Julie Larson with *Suburban Torture,* Marian Henley with *Maxine,* and, more recently, Nina Paley. In addition, there are over twenty-five tabloids devoted solely to comics throughout this country. Some, like *Funny Times,* are distributed nationally through subscriptions. Others, such as the *Austin Comic News* (Austin, Texas), or *Minne Ha! Ha!* (Minneapolis, Minnesota), are distributed locally. The comics carried by these publications are all self-syndicated, and are generally reprinted from the alternative weeklies.

Moreover, the work of self-syndicated lesbian cartoonists like Allison Bechdel

Some self-syndicated women cartoonists whose work appears in gay and lesbian papers. Top to bottom, Jennifer Camper, *Morgan Calabrese* by N. Leigh Dunlap, and *Sex, Religion & Politics,* by Angela Bocage, 1992.

Hawaii-based cartoonist Deb Aoki (top) and Flower Frankenstein (bottom right), from San Francisco's humor tabloid, *Harpoon,* 1992. Bottom left, *Stonewall Riots* by Andrea Natalie.

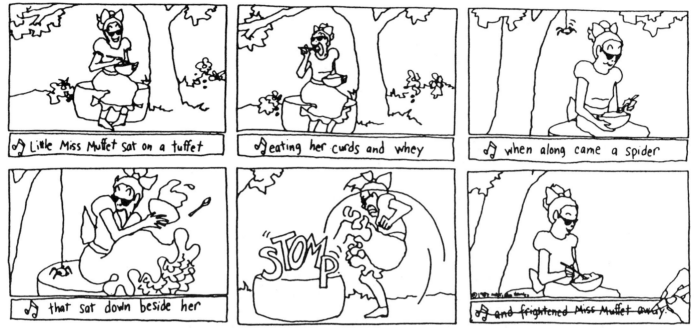

Little Miss Muffet sat on a tuffet

eating her curds and whey

when along came a spider

that sat down beside her

"STOP"

and frightened Miss Muffet away.

I dreamed I was taking the bus home from work only the bus was taking us to Paris for three weeks, and I had no choice but to leave the house and children in my husband's care.

Do you have any thoughts about what it might have meant?

Nationally-syndicated weekly strips. Top, Marian Henley; above, Gail Machlis.

(*Dykes to Watch Out For*), N. Leigh Dunlap (*Morgan Calabrese*), and Andrea Natalie (*Stonewall Riots*) can be found wherever gay and lesbian newspapers are carried.

There seems to be no reason why any number of women cartoonists should not be found on the comic pages of daily national newspapers, but this is not the case. I have counted exactly four strips by women cartoonists, none of which started more recently than the late 1970s: *Brenda Starr*, still going strong, and currently drawn by Ramona Fradon since Dale Messick's 1979 retirement; *Pogo*, now drawn by Walt Kelly's daughter Carolyn; and the two most recent, *Cathy* by Cathy Guisewite, and *For Better or For Worse*, by Lynn Johnston, both nearly 15 years old. There were ten strips drawn by women in the daily newspapers of 1942. Clearly, the situation has not improved. And yet, *women do read newspapers.*

For all women who either read or draw comics, the most encouraging event since Hilda Terry broke the sex barrier at the National Cartoonists Society, is the emergence of Barbara Brandon, the first nationally-syndicated black woman cartoonist since Jackie Ormes. (Since Ormes was syndicated in black newspapers only, Brandon may be considered the first to be truly nationally syndicated.) As a child,

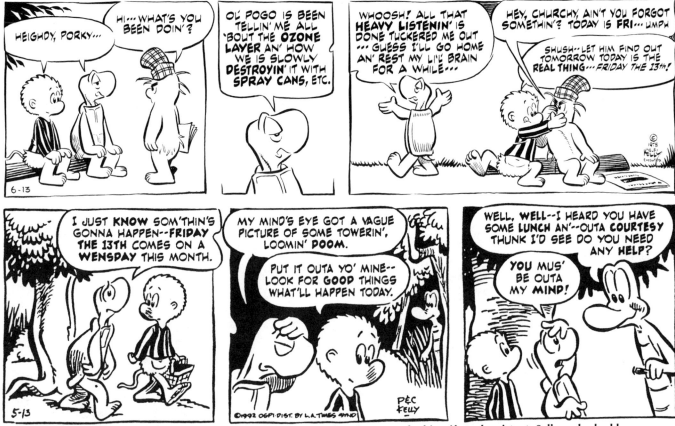

When *Pogo* creator Walt Kelly died in 1973, his strip was carried on for a year by his wife and assistant, Selby, who had been a Disney animator. She signed the strip "Selby Kelly, executrix." After almost a twenty-year hiatus, *Pogo* is now being drawn by Walt Kelly's daughter, Carolyn Kelly, and written by his son, Peter.

Brenda Starr, 1991. Since Dale Messick retired from the strip in 1970, the red-haired reporter has been drawn by Ramona Fradon.

Brandon learned about comics by assisting her father, Brumsick Brandon, Jr., creator of the prize-winning strip, *Luther.* Working in a Jules Feiffer-influenced style, she shares her strip, *Where I'm Coming From*, with her creations: a dozen or so black women, ranging in age from their early twenties to their early thirties, whose concerns go beyond fashion and weight loss. In one strip, Monica, a light-skinned woman, complains about her neighbor's attempts to pigeonhole her as "mulatto, quadroon or octoroon." She says, "What difference does it make? I'm black." In another strip, the same character says she is sick of people asking her,

Lyttle Women, 1990. This strip by Kathryn LeMieux was syndicated by King Features in 1990 and 1991.

Lynn Johnston's *For Better of For Worse*, 1992.

Cathy, 1992. Creator Cathy Guisewite makes an unusual (for the strip) political comment, drawn shortly before the 1992 presidential elections.

"What are you? You've got those green eyes and that long wavy hair. You can't be black...you must be mixed." Her answer is, "Yes I'm mixed. Try African American."

Brandon's father discontinued his strip in 1984, when distribution had dropped off so sharply that he felt it was no longer worth drawing it. In a 1991 article in the *Detroit Free Press*, Barbara Brandon comments, "In the late 1960s, everybody wanted a comic about blacks, by the end of the '70s, we were no longer a concern." However, the tide seems to have turned again. In an interview with

Lynn Johnston deals with homosexuality

When Lynn Johnston started this sequence dealing with homosexuality, in March, 1993, 20 newspapers cancelled her strip. Johnston had previously dealt with such subjects as child battering and anorexia, but newspaper editors, who seem to believe that the comic reading public prefers cat gags, felt that this time she went too far. During the 1988 presidential elections, Cathy Guisewite did a series of strips dealing with the problems a working mother encountered in a Republican administration. These, too, were cancelled by many papers. While Garry Trudeau can be, in fact, is *expected* to be, outspoken in *Doonesbury,* editors apparently want women cartoonists to stick to jokes about families and yuppie "career girls."

Above: Barbara Brandon, *Where I'm Coming From,* **1992.**

Right: Barbara Brandon

me, Brandon remarked dryly, "Black folks go in and out of vogue in this country."

Then she added something that could apply to all women cartoonists: "We're coming around to a point where they're ready to hear our voices again."

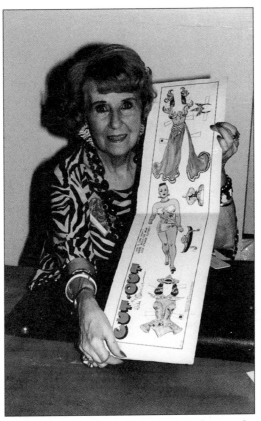

Still very much with us, Dale Messick, the grande dame of comics, displays one of her paper doll pages from the 1940s at a San Diego comic convention in the late 1980s.